Mary Ray's

SUPERDOG

Mary Ray's SUPERDOG

Clicker training for obedience, tricks and agility

Mary Ray
Andrea McHugh

hamlyn

An Hachette Livre UK Company
www.hachettelivre.co.uk

First published in Great Britain in 2008 by
Hamlyn, a division of Octopus Publishing Group Ltd
2–4 Heron Quays, London E14 4JP
www.octopusbooks.co.uk

ISBN 978-0-600-61700-6

A CIP catalogue record for this book is available from the British Library

Printed and bound in China

10 9 8 7 6 5 4 3 2 1

Contents

INTRODUCTION

This is the book that will help you and your dog achieve your maximum potential, whether in competition or simply when enjoying your family pet in the home and on walks together.

Using this book

The aim is to provide advice for people of all abilities and levels of experience. For example, breeders can discover what I consider to be the very best way of raising a puppy, while owners will be armed with the knowledge they need to find a breeder who raises their puppies in a way that gives them the very best start in life.

Here you will find detailed information and useful tips – even some of my best-kept secrets as to how I achieve such success with my dogs, whether in agility, heelwork to music or just amusing friends with the tricks my dogs are able to do. No matter what your goal, it all begins with a solid foundation of training, from the basics through to more advanced work. In the pages of this book you will find everything that you need to take you through all the different stages.

My own dogs

It has taken me a long time to accumulate the knowledge I now have. I married my husband, Dave, in 1978 and soon afterwards we got our first dog, a Lurcher called Sasha. She was lovely, but I had difficulty controlling her around other people – she loved everyone a bit too much! Then I discovered my local dog training club.

The first night I attended was a life-changing experience. I sat entranced, watching all the obedience and competition classes, and from that moment on I was completely hooked. I was determined to learn how to train my dogs properly and compete with them successfully. By the end of the 1980s I was head trainer of the club and am still actively involved,

training with my dogs every week. A good dog trainer never stops learning.

I bought my first superdog in 1979. He was a Border Collie called Mr Chips and he performed at the UK's top international dog show, Crufts, in 1984. Mr Chips then sired Red Hot Toddy, who was a very special dog and went on to win Crufts obedience with me. I only ever had to show Toddy something once and he understood – he was a born superdog. Since then I've been to Crufts every year, competing in agility and obedience and doing live, televised heelwork to music demonstrations.

Today, Dave and I share our home with nine superdogs. They all live in the house and have very normal lives, going for long walks every day and enjoying playing in the fields. They recognize me as the pack leader and are generally very happy dogs.

Throughout my career, I've won numerous top national awards and championships in both agility and obedience classes, but I can honestly say that I still get the same buzz from competing as I did back in the early days. I hope that you and your dog get as much satisfaction from training as I do, and that this book will motivate you to ensure your dog reaches his very own superdog potential.

Mary Ray

Good luck!

Catch your dog's attention with a click...

JUST CLICK!

The best way to train a superdog is with a clicker. Your dog quickly learns that a click marks the exact moment of a desired action and is always followed by a reward, so precise timing is vital. Think of the clicker as a mini-camera, used to try to capture a behaviour. Clicker training is always positive, so ignore unwanted behaviours as much as possible. You can also clicker train dogs in a group.

What is a clicker?

A clicker is a small, lightweight device with a metal tongue or button that emits a noise when pressed. The noise has an advantage over your voice, in that it is always consistent and carries no emotion for the dog to try to interpret. Practise with a clicker before using it near your dog, and remember that he has sensitive hearing so avoid close proximity to his head.

How clicker training works

- A clicker makes two noises: one when it is pressed down and one when it is released. This double click 'marks' your dog's behaviour, and the more competent you are with a clicker the more effective it will be.

- Clicker training is a form of what animal behaviourists term 'operant conditioning': each time you click, your dog hears it and realizes that whatever he has just done was correct. He then anticipates a reward.

- Food treats used as rewards can be fed directly from the hand or thrown out for your dog to pick up himself.

- Using a clicker encourages your dog to work out for himself what behaviour you want him to repeat. This can be a movement or a non-movement, such as walking or sitting still. A clicker is a very precise communication tool.

When training with a clicker everything must be very positive, so as far as possible unwanted behaviours are ignored. Superdogs are confident dogs and learn much more quickly when encouraged to work out for themselves what you want them to do.

Verbal commands

Throughout this book, there are references to verbal commands such as 'sit' or 'down'. However, for more advanced moves I always advise handlers to use a word that makes most sense to them. Only introduce a verbal command once your dog understands and is performing a desired behaviour. When you click and say your chosen word, he will associate the action with the command.

Use the sound of a double click to mark your dog's behaviour.

treats and rewards

Most dogs love food, and being natural scavengers are highly motivated to eat as much of it as possible at every opportunity. However, not all dogs have such a voracious appetite and you may have to do some detective work to discover what best motivates your dog during training.

Your dog should enjoy training with a toy.

payment or satisfaction and your dog is just the same, particularly if you want to train him to be a superdog.

Luring and clicker training

Food treats provide extra motivation and add to your dog's enjoyment during training sessions. Although it is possible to train your dog with food treats or toys without using a clicker (a technique known as luring – see pages 12–13), this takes longer and it will be more difficult for your dog to achieve superdog status. This is because without a clicker you cannot mark the *exact* moment a behaviour occurs, and by the time you feed a treat the behaviour has stopped. Combining luring with clicker training will help your dog learn much faster.

Food treats

Use a variety of treats, but make sure they are quite small as you will be using a lot. A treat should be tasty, have a

Which reward?

Some dogs will work for any food treats on offer, while others need higher value treats or will work better for the reward of playing with a favourite toy. Whichever reward or combination of rewards you use, be generous. Remember: you don't feel like working if you don't receive any

superdog treats

- Chicken pieces
- Ham
- Sausages or frankfurters
- Cooked liver and heart
- Cubes of mild, hard cheese
- Commercial low-calorie dog treats

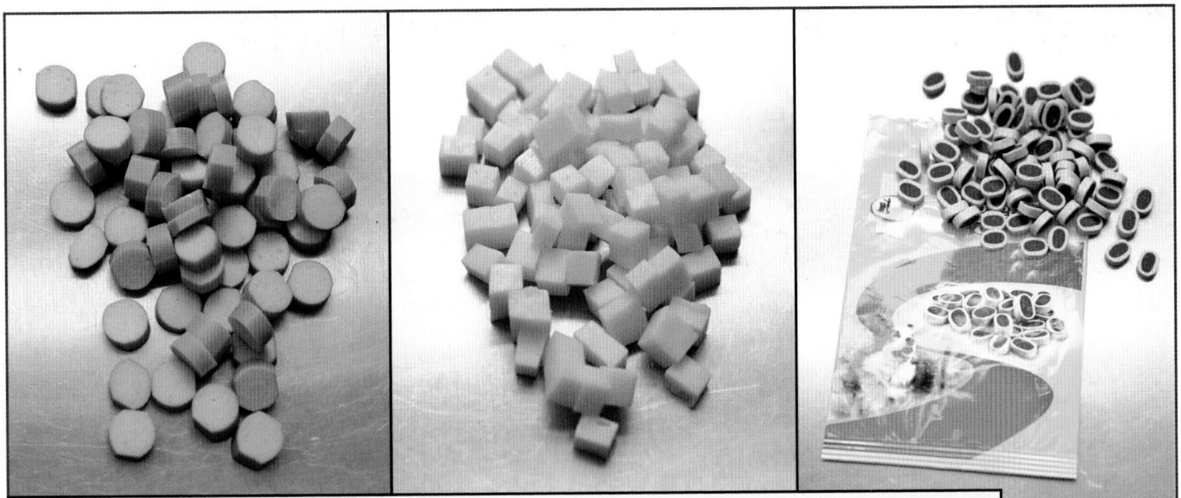

Variety is the spice of life, so use a selection of different training treats.

strong smell and, most importantly, be easy for your dog to eat. If he can't swallow it in three seconds, it's not a good training treat. Choose treats that also don't break up easily, as this helps to prevent your dog becoming distracted while he sniffs around for crumbs.

Chicken, ham and sausages are all favourites and ideal for everyday training sessions. Cooked liver and heart, or whatever is your dog's particular favourite, can be saved for times when you really need a superdog performance, such as preparing for a competition. Make sure you use treats that won't upset his digestive system. Commercial low-calorie training treats are a convenient option.

A superdog needs to be super fit to perform at his best, and carrying extra weight will cause problems for him. However, I have found that training treats don't cause weight gain as the dog burns off the extra calories while working.

Keep food treats and a clicker easily available all day, not just during training sessions. You never know when your dog will do something super for which you want to reward him.

super tip!

Carry treats in a dog trainer's waist bag or a pot with a tight-fitting lid. The best treat bags have a washable section for storing treats that can be removed and stored in the refrigerator ready for use the next day.

how superdogs learn

Even superdogs cannot learn to speak our language: his first language is body language. Your dog learns and communicates through watching the body language of other dogs, and also pays close attention to every move you make — not just during training sessions but throughout the day. Because your dog learns so much through observation, it is easier to begin training him by using a lure or signal and then attaching a verbal command when he is doing the action.

Luring

Do not think that because you are using a clicker you cannot lure your dog. I often do this, particularly if I want to shape the *way* a dog is doing something (see pages 34–35). The luring action eventually becomes the signal for a move, so, although you begin by luring several times with a treat (or toy), eventually you can dispense with this and the dog will respond to the signal.

Changing position

Practise luring your dog from one position to another by holding the treat higher so that he drops into a sit, clicking at the exact moment he sits. Experiment with your hand position and observe how this affects your dog's body position. Try luring him into a down position by taking the food down between his front feet and then drawing it back up again to get him into a sit.

Have a word

As well as the clicker, it is a good idea to use a word such as 'good' or 'yes', as this will be very useful when you don't have a clicker with you. Practise saying the word in a consistent manner, as unlike a clicker – which sounds the same every time you use it – unless you are extremely careful you can vary your tone and make a word sound different every time, which can easily confuse your dog.

super tip!

A superdog should follow the food carefully when he is being lured but not try to grab at it. To encourage this behaviour from the start, hold the treat in the end of your fingers, keep your hand still until your dog pulls his nose away, then click and give the treat. Your dog will learn that he gets the treat more quickly if he is patient.

simple luring

1 To begin luring, hold a food treat between your thumb and first two fingers so that your dog can see and smell it but cannot snatch it. Hold the treat out towards his nose and begin to walk in a circle with your dog on the outside – he will follow as he tries to sniff the food.

2 Continue to walk in a circle at a pace that maintains your dog's interest, so that he follows you without attempting to snatch the food, then click and feed the treat. If you move too slowly, he will try to nibble the food; if you move too fast, he will lose focus.

Target stick

A target stick gives you the advantage of an extension to your arm, which will produce greater movement from your dog. I have developed a target stick that has a clicker button on the handle and gives the dog a reward from a ball on the end, which opens. The dog will touch the target stick with his nose and follow with more drive and enthusiasm when he understands where the reward comes from.

what does a superdog need?

When it comes to superdogs, you get what you breed. If a puppy has very clever parents, he is likely to be a clever puppy. There will usually be some puppies in a litter that have a special star quality. Equally, one litter of puppies may all be brilliant, while another from a repeat mating may not.

Brainy breeds?

Although it is possible to train puppies that don't have the 'X factor', it is definitely easier to produce a superdog if you have a superpuppy to begin with, so go to a reputable breeder. In a perfect world, breed and brains will go together but this is not always the case. Breeds such as the Border Collie, that are still being bred for their working ability, are often more intelligent than other breeds that are now bred simply for their appearance.

Dogs can learn several different disciplines without becoming confused.

Try combining props with different moves.

Multi-tasking

A superdog can cope with more than one activity or discipline, and will benefit from and enjoy the variety of work given to him. For example, there is no reason why a dog cannot do heelwork to music *and* agility, and if he is trained carefully he can excel at both. You can use the same commands for different disciplines, such as 'weave' in heelwork to music and for the weaving poles in agility. However, it would not be advisable to ask your dog to weave through your legs if you were standing next to a set of weaving poles, as this would confuse him.

Loving it

You cannot force a dog to work, and he has to enjoy what he is doing in order to become a superdog. If he doesn't, this will be reflected in his performance.

A superdog is a pleasure to live with and to take out, because he can follow household rules and behave well among other dogs. It is unrealistic to think you will not have to correct your superdog from time to time, but you can usually do this simply by changing your vocal tone.

Although a lot of people are keen on learning behaviour techniques to help train their dogs, if you train your dog correctly from the start he will naturally accept you as the pack leader. If your dog does become over-dominant, you can employ behaviour techniques such as not allowing him through a door first and ensuring he is fed after you. However, with a correctly trained superdog this should not be necessary and in some cases may make him lose confidence, enthusiasm and motivation.

Downtime

Everybody needs a holiday occasionally and superdogs are no exception. From time to time, ensure your dog has a week or two with no training at all and you will find that he is much fresher and keener to learn new things when you start training again.

how to be a superdog trainer

A good handler has the knowledge and confidence to improve the way a dog works in training and competition. Equally, a poor handler can reduce the chances of even a superdog reaching his full potential. Discover here what it takes to become a superdog trainer.

Body language

In competitions such as agility, your dog will be working at speed off the lead and you will have to rely on your body language and voice to control him. It is therefore essential to think about how signals will be perceived by your dog. Be clear and consistent to minimize the risk of confusing him, and remember that he will tune into your silhouette so always try to keep your body shape clear.

Correct body language looks smarter and is easier for your dog to read.

Stay on side

The golden rule is always to use the hand nearest your dog to lure him or give visual signals. Using the hand that is further away means your arm crosses over your body and you may change your body direction slightly. This can confuse your dog, as your hand signal and body language may be giving him conflicting instructions.

In the early stages of training a move, you can make hand signals bigger and more exaggerated. When your dog understands what you want, gradually reduce them until he responds to quite subtle moves that are barely visible

Ten things a superdog trainer needs

1   Patience
2   Pack leader status
3   Confidence
4   Enthusiasm and energy
5   Clear body language
6   Consistency
7   Support and advice from another good trainer
8   Practical clothing and shoes
9   Abundant supply of high-value treats
10 Good sense of humour!

super tip!

A superdog trainer knows that they never stop learning. Find a good dog-training class with an instructor you trust and can relate to, and make time to attend regularly.

to an onlooker, although these must still be clear and easy for the dog to read.

Space invaders

If a puppy or small dog has not had the advantage of Early Neurological Stimulation (see pages 20–21) or been handled and socialized enough by the breeder, he may feel threatened by someone leaning over him. Kneeling down next to him can be less intimidating. When training, always make sure there is enough space for your dog to complete any move you are asking him to do.

Patience

During a training session, be consistent and patient. If you encounter problems, don't persist until your dog loses confidence – instead, go back a stage to something he understands and then gradually try to progress further. Always end a training session on a good note, praising your dog and making a fuss of him.

What to wear

Make sure your clothing is comfortable and suitable for the job at hand. Avoid tops with long, wide sleeves that may flap at your dog's eye level, long skirts, and anything that may restrict your movement or obstruct your dog.

Agility is a fast and furious sport so it is imperative you invest in a pair of good-quality, studded trainers designed for outdoor use that will help to prevent you slipping.

Puppies are never too young to learn.

SUPERPUPS

When it comes to superdogs, the breeder's role during those first important weeks of life cannot be overestimated. In this chapter, breeders can discover what I consider to be the very best way of raising a puppy, while owners will be armed with the necessary knowledge to find a breeder who raises puppies in a way that gives them the optimum start in life.

Learning programme

My favourite breeder is Bernadette Bay from the UK, who specializes in breeding Shetland Sheepdogs. Bernadette has developed an eight-week programme (outlined in this chapter) to ensure that when her puppies go to their new homes they already have a fantastic foundation of learning and socialization, and are well on their way to becoming superdogs.

This programme has been developed over 15 years of raising puppies, watching their development and evaluating performances in their chosen disciplines. The main focus is on raising agility and obedience dogs in the superdog league, but the programme is also entirely suitable for dogs not destined to compete. The goal is the same: to produce a puppy that is well socialized and eager to play. This is a puppy that has already learned that training is FUN.

Birth to two weeks

A puppy is born with his eyes and ears sealed shut. He has only his sense of touch and smell to help him find his mother to nurse and his littermates to cuddle for warmth. At this age, the puppy cannot even regulate his own body temperature or eliminate unaided.

The mother and her puppies should be allowed plenty of time undisturbed during this period. This is not the time for lots of noise and visitors, as the mother needs rest and relaxation in order to concentrate on her pups.

Early learning

The accepted practice of many breeders used to be to leave tiny puppies alone. Since they can't hear or see, why bother? Yet some studies have noted that early exposure to very mild stimulation helps puppies develop greater confidence and problem-solving ability as adults. This technique, known as Early Neurological Stimulation, involves some of the senses that tiny puppies do have – touch, position and temperature (see pages 20–21).

Young puppies snuggle together for warmth.

early neurological stimulation

According to Dr Carmen Battaglia, a highly respected expert on breeding dogs and a director of the American Kennel Club, the idea for Early Neurological Stimulation was first developed in the US military canine arena with the goal of producing a better working dog. Over the years various names have been applied to this method, including the Bio Sensor Program and the Superdog Program. Many breeders now use it on their litters in the hope of giving their puppies an advantage in their future training.

The five exercises

Dr Battaglia lists five important methods of stimulation that should be carried out with each puppy, starting on day three and ending around day 16. Perform each exercise for no longer than 5 seconds to avoid over stimulating your puppy.

Tickle between pads gently with a cotton bud.

Support your puppy with both hands when you hold him head up, tail down.

1 **Tickle toes** Lightly tickle the pup between and along the pads of his foot with a cotton bud for 3–5 seconds. You can tickle any foot and this can vary in each session. Some puppies wriggle more than others, so hold them securely.

2 **Head up, tail down** Hold the puppy with his head up and tail down for 3–5 seconds, supporting him in an upright position with both hands.

3 **Head down, tail up** Holding the puppy with both hands, rotate him so that his head is pointing downwards for 3–5 seconds.

4 **Belly up** Holding the puppy with both hands, lay him on his back with his belly facing upwards for 3–5 seconds. Some pups struggle more than others and you will need to be gentle yet firm.

5 **Cool off** Using a damp towel that has been cooled in the refrigerator for at least five minutes, place the puppy belly down onto the towel for 3–5 seconds. Allow him to move around or off the towel if he wants to.

Regular snuggle sessions are very important for your new pup.

Hold your puppy gently with his belly facing upwards.

Cuddle up

In addition to Early Neurological Stimulation techniques, the breeder should make time to hold each puppy a few times every day. Allowing him to snuggle against a person helps him to learn that human smell is associated with comfort. As the pups get older, the breeder can offer each one some yogurt or puréed baby food to lick off their fingers. This allows the puppy to begin to associate the smell of humans with things that taste good.

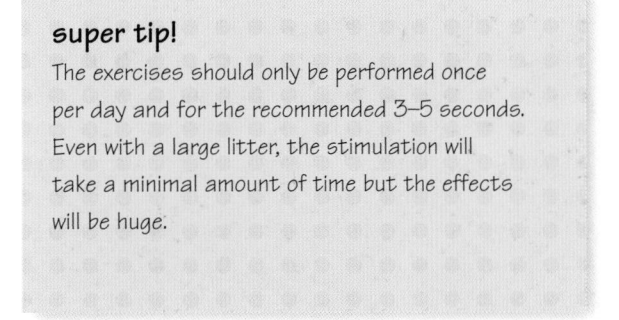

super tip!
The exercises should only be performed once per day and for the recommended 3–5 seconds. Even with a large litter, the stimulation will take a minimal amount of time but the effects will be huge.

two to five weeks

Once the puppies' eyes and ears open the breeder's real work in developing a superdog begins. There are many creative ways they can help the pups become accustomed to new sights, sounds and people.

Where the action is

Now is the time to move the puppies to the centre of activity in the house. This will provide daily exposure to general household noises such as the vacuum cleaner, washing machine, telephone, doorbell and television.

It is also good for the pups to see and hear children running and playing, and people going in and out of the house. The more varied the people they meet and have good experiences with, the friendlier the puppies will be as adults.

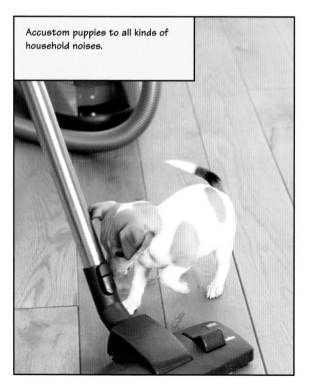

Accustom puppies to all kinds of household noises.

Easy listening

Set up a CD player near the puppy pen and softly play a selection of 'sound effects' CDs. The sounds can include thunder and lightning, fireworks, car noises and so on. Gradually build up the sound level to full volume to accustom the puppies to loud noises.

Good times to play CDs are when the puppies are nursing or are out of the pen playing together. During these times they will be relaxed and happy and will easily become accustomed to strange noises.

Toy time

Once the pups are up and moving on their own, you can start adding toys for them to explore. Toys that move, light up and make sounds help them to feel confident about things moving underfoot and producing sudden noises.

Inexpensive children's toys can be found in charity shops and at garage sales. Baby tunnels and cardboard boxes are fun for the pups to run around and hide in. Soft toys hanging from the puppy pen are great to encourage tugging play. Some breeders hang musical baby mobiles over the puppy pen to encourage the pups to look up and become used to flapping noises overhead.

One to one

Individual play can be introduced as early as three weeks and is one of the most important things the breeder can do to produce a puppy that loves to interact with people. The pups should be handled individually away from their littermates four to six times a day. It may be just sitting on a lap while watching television, playing tuggie (see pages 36–37) on the kitchen floor, carrying the pup around while doing housework or going outside to collect the mail. Creativity is essential when raising a superdog! Individual playtime helps to develop confidence and increase a puppy's desire to work with his owner one to one.

Keep the sessions short: there is no substitute for the knowledge that pups gain from their mother and littermates, so the bulk of their time should be spent together. A well-adjusted mother will teach her puppies many positive things, so as a potential superpup buyer you should evaluate her temperament as a dog's future behaviour is developed from a combination of genetics and environment.

Playing with a variety of toys will make your puppy more confident.

five to eight weeks

Puppies of this age are very active. They are starting to be weaned slowly from their mother – most breeders give her more time away from the pups at this stage, but she will usually be with them at night and a few times each day.

Busy breeder!

During this particularly busy period, when there is always so much feeding and clearing up to be done, the breeder must still take time to ensure that the puppies' socialization and training programme continues regardless. Individual playtime sessions should be increased and busy breeders will enlist the help of friends and relatives to help give their puppies the very best possible start in life.

More play

New items can be given to the pups for them to explore. Cardboard boxes make great mountains to climb; skateboards are brilliant as puppies can feel what it's like when something moves under their feet. Outdoor plastic children's climbing toys are great for an outdoor puppy playpen, encouraging the pups to climb, play and learn to use their bodies in new ways. All these experiences will make them bolder as they get older.

Click a trick

Starting a puppy on clicker training at around five weeks of age will be of great benefit to the new owner. The treats can be soft cheese or baby food that the pup can lick off the handler's fingers, and tiny pieces of cooked mincemeat are easy for him to chew. Puppies quickly learn that a 'click' means a treat is coming.

The pups can be played with individually a few times each day with a goal of teaching an easy 'trick' such as sit or down, shake a paw and spin right or left. Teaching them to push a mini-skateboard is always fun, too.

The sole aim is to teach the young pups to use their brains and enjoy

Introduce your puppy to toys that move to make them bolder.

learning. It doesn't matter *what* you teach, as long as they learn that it's fun to 'work' with people. A clicker encourages a puppy to think for himself and offer new behaviours without fear of being 'wrong'. This will boost his confidence and help him to feel secure when working with people.

Tug and toy play

Having a dog that loves tugging and toys will make training easier. At this young age, most puppies of all breeds will play tug and retrieve games with people, but if this enthusiasm is not gently encouraged it can easily be lost.

The breeder should take each puppy into a separate area at least once a day and spend two or three minutes playing retrieve and tug games. They should keep sessions short and not throw the toy very far, as puppies have a short attention span. The pups will begin to learn that playing with people can be as much fun as playing with other dogs. If you are hoping to train a superdog in agility or obedience, get one that is already keen on playing tug and retrieve games with people.

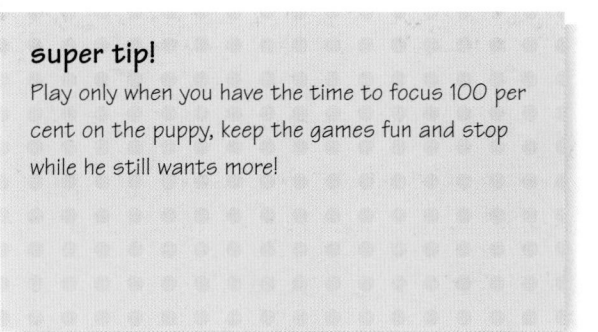

super tip!
Play only when you have the time to focus 100 per cent on the puppy, keep the games fun and stop while he still wants more!

Playing tuggie can teach pups that people can be as much fun to play with as other dogs.

social animals

Socialization is a very important issue with any breed of puppy, and particularly one that is destined to become a superdog. From five weeks of age until the pup is ready to go off to his new home, socialization should be a primary focus for the breeder.

Visiting hours

Arranging visits from a variety of people should continue, so that the puppies begin to associate strangers with good things. This is also a good time for you to pay regular visits, so that your puppy begins to develop positive associations with you – his new owner!

Exploration

The puppies should gradually be introduced to different areas of the house and garden, under supervision. You do not want a puppy that has only had experience of one room in a house, as he will be less confident about exploring new environments when you bring him home.

Visiting your puppy at the breeder's will help to develop a positive relationship early on.

Bonding

According to studies of canine behaviour, the ideal time for a pup to bond with humans is between six and eight weeks of age. It is imperative that the breeder understands this and actively works with their puppies to encourage such a bond to develop. Puppies should not be left all day with their littermates, only seeing humans when it is feeding time.

New experiences

Studies have also shown that a puppy should be introduced to a wide variety of experiences before the age of 12 weeks. This is the time when he is most adaptable and accepting of new things. Research shows that puppies kept in a kennel until 16 weeks of age are less adaptable and more timid – definitely not superdog material!

Most breeders today do not keep their puppies in kennels, but it is still just as important for them to remember to vary a pup's exposure to new experiences.

Time out

Puppies can be taken out for short journeys in a car. This not only introduces them to the motion of the vehicle but also allows them to experience new sights and sounds.

A trip to the local superstore is a good option. The back of the car can be opened up and the pups (with their mother at first) can watch the comings and goings in the busy store car park from the safety of a travel crate.

Eventually, at around six to seven weeks of age, the puppies can be carried around near the store to allow some interaction with strangers. The noise of the shopping trolleys and the general hustle and bustle of the store will all be completely new to them. They should be encouraged to observe these new distractions and be given treats and verbal praise if needed – whatever will make the outing successful for them. The idea is not to scare the puppies but to keep them in a happy and relaxed state of mind.

Take short journeys with your puppy to get him used to travelling.

pens, crates and home time

The later stages of your puppy's time at his breeder's home will help to determine how easy he is to house-train in the future. An invaluable tool for any puppy owner is a puppy crate, which your new little superdog will soon come to view as his own special den.

Clean beginnings

The way the breeder sets up the puppy pen can help to make house training much easier once the puppy is in his new home. Giving the pups an area away from their sleeping box will encourage them to eliminate away from their bed. Most breeders start by opening up the whelping box into a larger pen filled with several sheets of newspaper. The pups sleep in the whelping box but can easily walk out to eliminate on the paper.

As the puppies grow, the pen is expanded. One good method is to take out the whelping box and replace it with the bottom of one or two plastic travel crates (according to the breed of puppy and size of the litter). The puppies will start to use the crate to sleep in and eliminate outside it.

When you are busy put your puppy in a pen to play happily with his toys.

Your puppy will enjoy exploring the sights and smells of the garden.

Additionally, in good weather the pups can usually be encouraged to eliminate outside during outdoor playtime.

Crate training

At around six to seven weeks of age the breeder can also get the puppies started on crate training. The first step is to add the top (without the door) to the crate inside the puppy pen. The pups will enjoy their little den. Then, during occasional naptimes, the pups can be put in a closed crate outside the puppy pen, two or three at a time to start with and then eventually alone. It is important that these crate times are kept short, to avoid the pups eliminating in their crate.

Soon the puppies will learn that the crate is a safe and secure place in which to sleep and relax. This will help the new owner when the puppy needs to be confined for safety in a car, or at night to help with house-training.

Leaving home

Depending on the breed, puppies are usually ready to go to their new homes at between seven and nine weeks of age, in order that their superdog training can begin as early as possible. Some breeds will mature earlier than others and it is best to discuss the exact date with your breeder in advance.

Hopefully, by the time your puppy is ready to 'leave home' he will have been exposed to many different situations, sounds and people. He will also have been introduced to a collar and lead, be crate trained and have been taught at least one trick. He will have learned some basic manners, picked up some idea about house training, and been encouraged to tug and retrieve as much as possible – toy drive is an important part of training a performance dog. With these beginnings, your new puppy will have a great head start towards becoming a superdog.

Home time is when the fun begins!

HOME TIME!

Bringing your superpup home will always be an exciting time, but forward planning and attention to detail is essential to ensure that his transition from the breeder's home to yours is as smooth and stress-free as possible.

Medical matters

When you bring your puppy home at between seven and nine weeks of age, he should already have had his worming treatments. Make arrangements for a check-up with your vet, so that he can have his vaccinations and you can ask for further worming advice.

Ask for details

Find out how much work the breeder has done with your puppy to prepare him for the big, wide world. Responsible breeders will already have embarked on an extensive socialization programme, but you should ask about exactly what has been done to get your pup used to other people, noises and distractions in the home.

Buy everything you need for your puppy before bringing him home.

Ask also whether he has ever been for a short journey in a car. If not, the journey to his new home may be the first time your puppy has travelled, so do everything you possibly can to make this a positive experience for him. Arrange to pick up your pup before he has been fed and allow plenty of time for the journey, so that you are as calm as possible on arrival. Make sure you have a suitable carry cage or puppy crate for him to travel in, and perhaps put a blanket over the top to encourage him to sleep through the journey.

Be prepared

In the weeks before your puppy's arrival, shop for all the things he is going to need, which include:

- Puppy pen
- Bed and blankets
- Towels
- Food and water bowls
- Collar and lead
- Toys
- Dog food
- Grooming kit
- Clicker

In addition, it's a good idea to collect a large pile of old newspapers, which can be very useful during your puppy's house-training period. Stock up on the same puppy food as the breeder used, as sudden changes can upset his digestion. Make any changes to his diet gradually.

superdog routines

You will need to establish a routine for your puppy to help him feel safe and secure. Start as you mean to go on as regards his behaviour, as it is easier to teach a dog correctly from the beginning than to retrain him later on.

House-training

The first weeks of puppy ownership are very tiring and you will have to take him outside frequently. Watch for signs that he might want to relieve himself: his nose may go down and his tail up. Accidents are inevitable but don't get upset – simply clean up and start again. You can gradually introduce a verbal command such as 'hurry up' to encourage your pup. If he urinates when he greets you,

Young puppies need to be taken outside frequently during house-training.

your puppy is being submissive and it is important not to reprimand him but to try to concentrate on increasing his confidence instead.

Mealtimes

Schedule puppy training before feeding, so that your puppy works well for the treats you offer.

Exercise

It's up to you whether you take your puppy out for pre-vaccination exercise, but if not you can still carry him so that he gets used to meeting people and experiencing new sights and sounds. I walk my new puppies in a safe place at eight weeks and also let them off the lead, as at that age they will happily follow without wandering off. Get into the habit of calling your puppy's name and giving a treat when he comes.

Start getting your puppy used to wearing a lightweight lead in the house and, if you notice him following you, pick it up. When out with other dogs, keep your puppy on an extendable flexi-lead to give him some freedom yet ensure he doesn't over-exercise and damage his joints.

Grooming

Your puppy must learn to accept and enjoy being groomed, so begin when he is sitting quietly on your knee and is feeling happy and relaxed. You may find that a grooming table is a great investment as many dogs fidget less when standing on one.

Dogs are more relaxed about grooming on a grooming table and the added height makes it easier for the handler.

Trust me

It's important for your puppy to develop trust in you. As soon as anyone verbally or physically abuses a puppy, the trust is broken. Be patient, and remember that your pup needs you to teach him what you want him to do.

Pens and crates

Keep a puppy pen in your main living area so that your pup can be part of the family and safely play without you worrying that he might chew something he shouldn't. Chewing and mouthing are natural puppy behaviours and to discourage them entirely can make him reluctant to do some superdog activities, such as retrieving. Line an area of your puppy pen with newspaper, so that if he has an accident it is easy to clean up and your puppy will not become anxious.

A crate makes a perfect puppy bedroom and should be a safe, cosy den for your pup to sleep or stay in when you have to go out. Some people are horrified at the idea of shutting a puppy in a crate, but it is far worse to come home and shout at or physically punish a puppy for chewing or toileting in the wrong place.

target training for superdogs

Introduce your dog to the various aspects of target training and you will be surprised at how quickly he will understand how to use different parts of his body for different targets.

target stick

1 A target stick can teach your dog to move at different paces and in a specific direction. A stick that gives a reward from the ball on the end can be a very effective motivator. Hold the stick towards your dog and, when his nose touches it to sniff, click and treat.

2 Now begin to move the target stick, so that your dog learns to follow it and click him for either nose touching or following. When he is motivated to follow the target stick you can teach him how you want him to move, i.e. in a trot. You can also incorporate the other moves, such as a twist, bow or creep. The behaviour should also transfer to a prop, such as a dancing cane.

Clicker basics

- Your dog should ALWAYS get at least one reward when you click, but being unpredictable with the number of rewards will keep him sharp.
- Be generous with treats, but only click ONCE.
- If you are teaching something challenging, use higher-value treats.
- Be patient: allow your dog time to work out what you want.
- Perfect your timing: you only get what you click for!

Click and carry on

Many people think that a click always ends a behaviour, but this is not necessarily true. For example, when practising heelwork your dog will be much more attentive if you click *before* a turn and then treat *afterwards*. On hearing the click your dog will become very alert and you can then maintain his attention through the turn. Remember that you click for a stay or wait, and return to your dog then treat.

target marker

1 Use a target marker to tell your dog to go to a specific place or touch an item with his nose or paw. Place a treat on a plastic lid, then encourage him to get it, clicking as his nose touches the marker. Repeat several times and give a verbal command as you click. If your dog touches the marker, click and throw a treat away from the target, then repeat. Now try without a treat on the marker, clicking and rewarding if he touches it. If not, continue putting down treats until he understands.

2 For paw work, use a larger mat. Place a treat on the side of the mat furthest from him. Encourage him to get the treat, clicking as he steps onto the mat. Repeat several times, then introduce a verbal command as you click. Now try without a treat on the mat, clicking and rewarding if he stands on the mat. If not, continue putting down treats until he understands. You can also teach the down on a mat.

playing tuggie

Many people think that encouraging your dog to play tuggie is not to be recommended as it may create problems with aggression. However, provided he is properly trained it is important that your superdog is encouraged to use his mouth.

Tuggie skills

In obedience, your dog will need to use his mouth for exercises such as retrieve and scent, as well as for tricks such as wrapping himself in a blanket (see pages 116–117).

Teaching your dog to 'leave' a toy on command and swap it for a treat will enable you both to enjoy a game of tuggie, and this can be a great motivational training tool.

If your dog is not keen on playing close to the hand try using a longer tuggie.

Teaching tuggie

When you throw a toy for a dog that has not yet learned to retrieve, he may or may not bring it back to you. Tuggie is different, as it encourages your dog to interact with you and be confident about coming in close, holding something in his mouth and pulling against you. Hopefully, the breeder will already have taught your puppy to play tuggie, but if not it is a good idea to do this as soon as you can.

Encouraging your dog

Some dogs are not keen to play close to their owner's hand, and if this is the case with yours try using a longer tuggie toy such as a long knotted fleece, so that you can gradually reduce the distance between you. Because clicker training is so non-physical, you can also take the opportunity to get your dog used to being handled by occasionally giving him a stroke or pat while still holding the tuggie.

A puppy needs a tuggie toy on which he can get a good grip and that is nice and soft in his mouth. Some breeds with softer mouths – such as Shelties, Greyhounds or Whippets – may not want to use their mouth, and teething puppies may not be keen to play tuggie either. If this is the case, try using a lightweight cat toy to bring out the prey drive – most dogs find these irresistible!

Leave it!

When playing with the tuggie, give your dog a command such as 'give it' or 'leave it', clicking and treating each time he complies.

Patience, please

To be a superdog your puppy will need plenty of basic training, which is covered in detail in the next chapter. However, from the very early stages when you are playing with him or teaching a behaviour it is a good idea

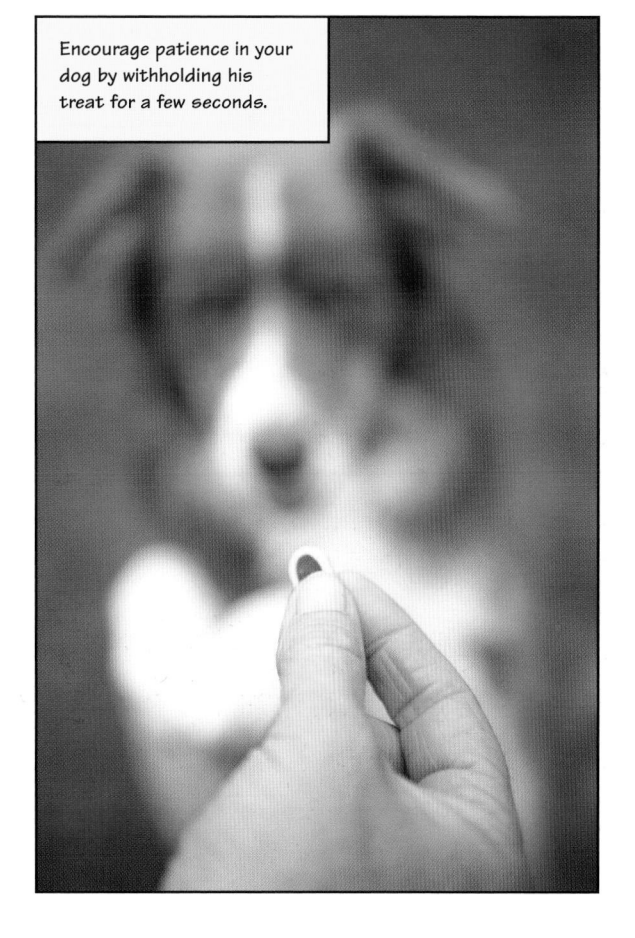

Encourage patience in your dog by withholding his treat for a few seconds.

occasionally to click and withhold the treat for a few seconds before you feed it to him. This slight hesitation will teach your puppy to be patient, which is a valuable lesson to learn early on in trainng.

superdog recalls

Recall is one of the tests your dog will be expected to perform in an obedience competition. However, it is a valuable lesson for any dog to learn. There is nothing more infuriating than taking your dog out for a walk and having him totally ignore you when you want him to come back.

Making a start

Begin recall training early. Allow your puppy to run on in front of you, then call his name and click as he turns towards you. Always carry some delicious treats with which to reward him, and give liberal praise when he gets to you. *Never* shout at him if he doesn't come back, or smack him when he finally does, as he'll be even more reluctant to return the next time. Avoid chasing your pup as he will think this a great game – it is much more effective to run away from him.

All in a name

When you call your dog to you, you will usually call his name – so when choosing a name be careful that it doesn't clash with any of your training commands. For example, one of my superdogs is called Levi, but I soon realized that this name was easily confused with the 'leave it' command, so for that particular dog I use the word 'give' instead.

Give your dog lots of praise and a reward when he returns to you.

super tip!

Try to choose a name that doesn't sound too 'flat', to which you can give meaning to express approval or disapproval. I have found that names with a 'y' on the end give more opportunity for greater inflection. Beware, too, of accent and dialect – some names sound lovely in one accent but are not as attractive or easy to say in another.

Teaching your puppy to come

Carry plenty of treats and a clicker, and wait until your puppy is a few steps away before calling his name. If necessary, rustle your treat bag to get his attention. As soon as he turns to look at you, click. Your puppy will already know that a click means reward, so will come to you to get a treat.

Repeat several times, then call your puppy's name and add on the command 'come'. Click as he comes towards you and treat him as soon as he sits in front of you. When your puppy can do this fluently, you can teach him to finish in the heel position. You can then progress to the recalls he will need in obedience competitions (see box right).

obedience test recalls

Novice The handler leaves the dog in a sit or down, walks away in a straight line and about turns before halting and calling the dog. The dog joins the handler, sits in front and finishes in the heel position.

A-test The dog is left in a sit or down, the handler walks away in a pattern directed by the steward or judge, and then calls the dog. The dog joins the handler in the heel position and they then move together until told to halt.

competitive recall

1 To achieve a faster recall, ask a helper to hold your puppy by his collar and walk away, then turn back and call him.

2 When your pup is released he should come running towards you. When he reaches you, give him lots of praise and rewards.

Practise a little give and take in training.

THE BASIC SKILLS

When a handler and dog are working well together there seems to be a perfect, silent communication between them – as if the dog really understands what his handler is thinking and is only too pleased to do whatever is asked of him. Of course, all this may look effortless but you can be sure handler and dog have worked on the basics for months and sometimes years.

Starting to train

This chapter covers the basics of training. You should spend as long as it takes to perfect each stage before moving on to the next. As well as working with your dog at home, it is a good idea to enrol in a training class at a reputable club. Not only will you benefit from professional advice, but your dog will learn to cope with the sights, smells and distractions of other dogs. A superdog must always remain focused on what his handler is asking him to do.

Mini-lessons

Outside your training sessions, there are always many opportunities throughout the day to give your dog mini-lessons that help to reinforce what he has already learned.

Keep a treat bag handy at all times so that you can reward your dog whenever he does something new or exceptionally well. For example, place a pot of tasty treats in a visible spot in the hall and each time a visitor comes to the door tell your dog to go to his bed, then ask the visitor to feed him a treat. This will help your dog to build positive associations with visitors arriving and you will soon find that when he hears the doorbell he will go straight to his bed, in anticipation of receiving a treat.

Similarly, before you put your dog on the lead to go out for a walk ask him to sit. When you return, ask him to lie down so that you can examine his feet for grass seeds. All these mini-lessons are very useful in real-life situations, but they will also help to make your dog much more obedient if you decide you would like to have a go at competitions.

Ensure your dog will sit calmly before you walk him.

the four commandments

Everything your superdog will need to know comes from the four basic commands: sit, stand, down and wait. Begin working on these as soon as possible – even a small puppy is capable of understanding and learning them and will soon be well on his way to becoming a superdog.

sit

Call your dog and hold a treat in front of his nose. Now raise the treat up and back over his head until he drops into a sit, then click and reward. Repeat several times, then introduce the word 'sit' as his hindquarters drop.

down from sit

With your dog in a sit, hold a treat under his nose. His nose and head will lower. Slowly lure him diagonally forward and down and, as he goes down, click and reward. Repeat several times, saying 'down' as he drops his front end.

stand from sit

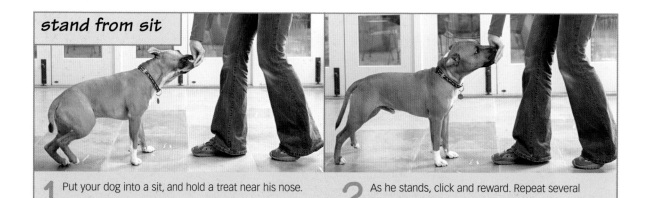

1 Put your dog into a sit, and hold a treat near his nose. Step back, slowly pulling the treat towards you, but level with your dog's nose.

2 As he stands, click and reward. Repeat several times, saying 'stand' as he raises his hindquarters.

Wait

1 There is a subtle difference between the 'wait' and 'stay' commands. 'Wait' means your dog must wait in position until you tell him to do something else, while 'stay' means he should stay where he is until you return.

It's easier to teach your dog to wait when he is in a sit. If he is taught to resist slightly when he feels a pull on his lead, this will also help to prevent him breaking the move, which is very useful in obedience and agility. Begin with your dog on the lead in a sit, then click and reward. Now click again and wait a few seconds before rewarding. Repeat a few times, gradually increasing the time before rewarding. Now step back and pull slightly on the lead. If your dog feels this and resists slightly, click.

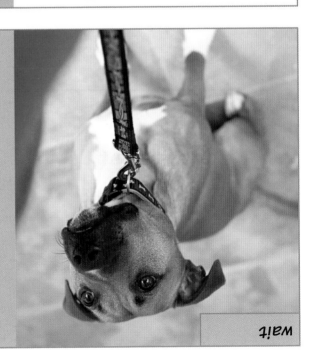

2 Gradually increase the pressure but don't jerk the lead, clicking when your dog resists. Say 'wait' as you feel him do this. Soon you can take more steps away and say wait, then click, return (releasing the pressure on the lead as you do so) and reward. If your dog breaks the sit after the click, put him back into a sit and reward but don't click again. When he doesn't break position on hearing the click but waits for you to return to the heel position, reward him. This is an example of the click not ending the behaviour – the reward does. Now give a release command such as 'OK', which indicates to your dog that the exercise has finished and he can leave his spot. When your dog has learned to wait in sit you can train in the same way in a down and a stand.

basic heelwork

Being able to walk with your dog off the lead in the 'at heel' position will be useful in all aspects of your daily life. Moving smartly into the heel position will also help your dog to develop back-end awareness, which is something that he will need as his training progresses.

Heelwork in competition

For obedience heelwork you need only teach the heel position on your left side, but for heelwork to music, freestyle or agility you will need to teach it on both sides. In agility, the advantage is that when you set up your dog at the start you won't have to handle him too much, as he will know exactly where to go. In addition, when things go wrong you can bring him back to heel or side easily.

At heel on the move

Practise walking with your dog at heel in circles, serpentines and figures of eight. Hold a treat at your side so your dog has to look up at you.

Start by walking a right circle, which is easier for your dog as you are not walking into him. Gradually change to a left circle, so that he is now on the inside of you.

Teach your dog to walk at heel on your right in exactly the same way, but use a different command.

teaching at heel

1 Clicker training is the quickest way to teach your dog to swing into the heel position, because the accuracy of the click as he uses his back legs is unmistakable. Begin with your dog standing in front of you, slightly off-centre to your left. Keep your feet together and hold a treat in an overhand position, level with his nose.

3 Now put your feet together and treat when your dog sits straight at the side of you. His nose should be close to your left knee. Repeat on both sides, saying 'close' just prior to clicking. Now stop luring: hold a treat behind your leg, use the verbal command and click as your dog swings his back end around. Finally, hold the treat where you want his nose to be and as soon as he hears the word 'close' he should immediately swing his back end around and get into position. Once your dog understands this, when he gets into position hold the treat high so that he automatically drops into a sit.

2 Step back with your left foot and lure your dog behind you with the treat, then lure him back again in an anti-clockwise arc. Holding the treat behind your leg, encourage him to really swing around and into position. Click as he moves his back end around.

in front

The 'in front' command means your dog stands directly in front of you, while the 'come' command (see pages 38–39) means he sits directly in front of you. This move is particularly important if you want to try heelwork to music, as it forms the basis for many dance routines.

Advantages

Teaching the in front position will make your dog become back-end aware and enables you to straighten him from a distance. It is also useful if you teach your dog to walk back, as if he goes off line you can easily straighten him.

There are two ways to teach the in front position. Try both methods to see which one is the most effective for positioning your dog. Once he understands what you are asking him to do, you should be able to move from side to side and he will move with you.

method 1

1 Hold some treats in one hand and a clicker in the other, at waist level. Position your hands as if clasped together. Your dog will soon associate this as a visual signal for 'in front'. Click when he is directly in front of you.

2 Instead of giving your dog a treat, throw it out about 2 m (6 ft) to the side of him so that he has to go and get it.

super tip!

Your dog will generally find this exercise easier on one side than the other, so practise equally on both sides. Although the 'in front' command is normally taught by throwing food away from you, slower dogs may respond faster if you click and reward in front, and then throw food out to the side.

method 2

1 Encourage your dog to step his front legs up onto a low step. Position your hands as in method 1, as a visual signal for 'in front'. Click and reward for keeping his front legs on the step.

3 When he comes back, at first he will probably stop at an angle, but click and reward as he steps to bring his body around to stand straight in front of you. Practise throwing a treat to either side, then introduce the words 'in front' to cue the move. To encourage your dog to return quickly and stand straight, withhold the click until he learns that it is how he returns and stands that earns him the treat.

2 Move around the step and your dog should move his back legs to maintain position. Click and reward as your dog moves his back end around. Repeat several times, then introduce the 'in front' command to cue the move and dispense with the step.

look and learn

A superdog needs to be able to focus on you all the time, but also on other objects when asked to. For example, if you are sending him away to a target mat or to retrieve something, he needs to know where you want him to go without lots of unnecessary pointing and arm waving. For this, you need to teach him the 'look' command.

Watch me

Most of the time your dog will be observing you naturally – when you pick up a handful of treats, get his food bowl or grab his lead.

In an obedience competition or freestyle heelwork to music, if this is your aim, your dog has to be watching and focusing on you all the time. Even in agility, where you want his head to be facing forward and not turning to watch you intensely, he will still be watching you with his peripheral vision.

To help develop this on command, the next time you do something and notice that your dog is watching you, put the 'watch' command to it. Your dog will soon learn what the word means.

Hands on

With clicker training, your hands will be off your dog for a lot of the time, but there are occasions when holding him by the collar can help to motivate him. Teaching the 'look' command is one of these instances.

First, you need to get your dog accustomed to being held by his collar. If you don't do this, he may develop a habit of avoiding being held, or even become fearful or resentful of it.

To teach your dog to accept being held, put your hand on his collar, then click and treat him. This is why the clicker works so well as a training tool, because you are able to click at exactly the moment your hand goes onto his collar.

look!

1 To start, get your dog in the close position and hold his collar.

super tip!

Don't start pointing your hand or using meaningless hand signals towards something you want your dog to look at, as logically he will look at your hand and not in the direction you are pointing. Instead, teach him to look on command.

4 Then click and release his collar. The toy or treat that he goes to fetch will become his reward. Eventually, you will be able to give the 'look' command without holding his collar, and then progress to putting the 'look', and 'wait', commands together.

3 As your dog watches where it lands, say 'look'.

2 Now throw a toy or treat, not too far away.

do the twist!

Teaching your dog to twist – turn a tight circle to the right or left – is useful in agility competitions and if you want to try your hand at freestyle heelwork to music. It will also help to get your dog supple in both directions.

Before you start

Your dog should already be aware of the 'in front' command (see pages 46–47), and you will have practised moving with him in different directions as he maintains the in front position.

Your hands will signal the direction in which you want him to twist: use your left hand as a signal to twist to the left, and your right hand for him to twist to the right. Think of swimming the breaststroke – your right hand always circles clockwise and your left hand anticlockwise.

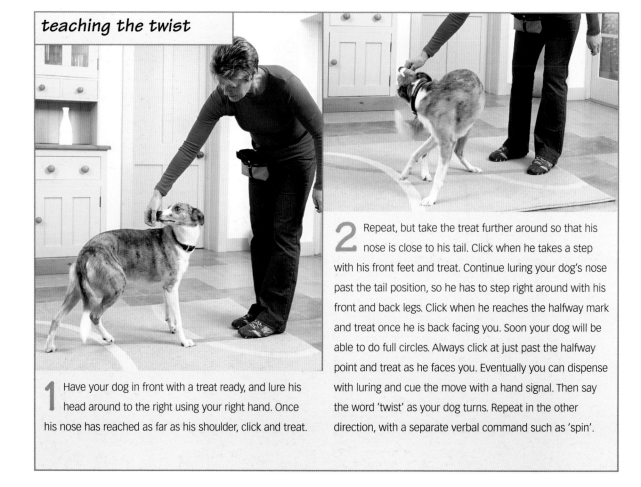

teaching the twist

1 Have your dog in front with a treat ready, and lure his head around to the right using your right hand. Once his nose has reached as far as his shoulder, click and treat.

2 Repeat, but take the treat further around so that his nose is close to his tail. Click when he takes a step with his front feet and treat. Continue luring your dog's nose past the tail position, so he has to step right around with his front and back legs. Click when he reaches the halfway mark and treat once he is back facing you. Soon your dog will be able to do full circles. Always click at just past the halfway point and treat as he faces you. Eventually you can dispense with luring and cue the move with a hand signal. Then say the word 'twist' as your dog turns. Repeat in the other direction, with a separate verbal command such as 'spin'.

teaching the half twist

1 Hold a treat in each hand and position your dog on your right.

2 Use your right hand as a signal to turn him away from you. At the same time, do a right about turn.

Half twist

When your dog is in close, if you and he both twist a complete circle you will both end up facing in the same direction as you started. In a half twist, you and your dog end up facing in the opposite direction to where you started. Half twists are very useful for agility, as you can turn your dog away from you. In freestyle heelwork, you can change his position from on your left to on your right.

3 Your dog is now on your left and you treat him with your left hand. With your dog starting on your left, reverse these instructions. If you stand still and signal a half twist in one direction and then the other, you can move your dog in a figure of eight.

round in circles

Here your superdog learns how to circle closely around you and then to make a wider circle. This move is taught by luring with a toy or treat – the key is to ensure you transfer the lure from hand to hand quickly. Any hesitation can make your dog falter or stop, and will confuse him.

circling close

1 If you have a small dog, start by bending down. Once he is following the lure well you can stand up. With your dog in close, hold a toy plus a clicker in your right hand, and lure him across the front of you.

2 To move your dog around the back, lure from one hand to the other. As soon as he is following your left hand, click. Treat when he returns to the left heel position.

3 Keep practising, offering treats at different points on the circle. Introduce the command 'round' and gradually dispense with treats and then the hand signals. Soon you can stop using hand signals as well.

Opposing circles

Once your dog is fluent on a circle around you and knows the verbal command, try turning the opposite way to him: if he is circling around to the right, you turn and on the spot circle to the left. This will act as a visual signal to cue the move.

super tip!

Lungeing a horse in a circle helps to exercise him and keep him supple and well balanced. Practising circling with a dog works in much the same way and is very useful in agility. It is important to practise equally in both directions.

circling wide

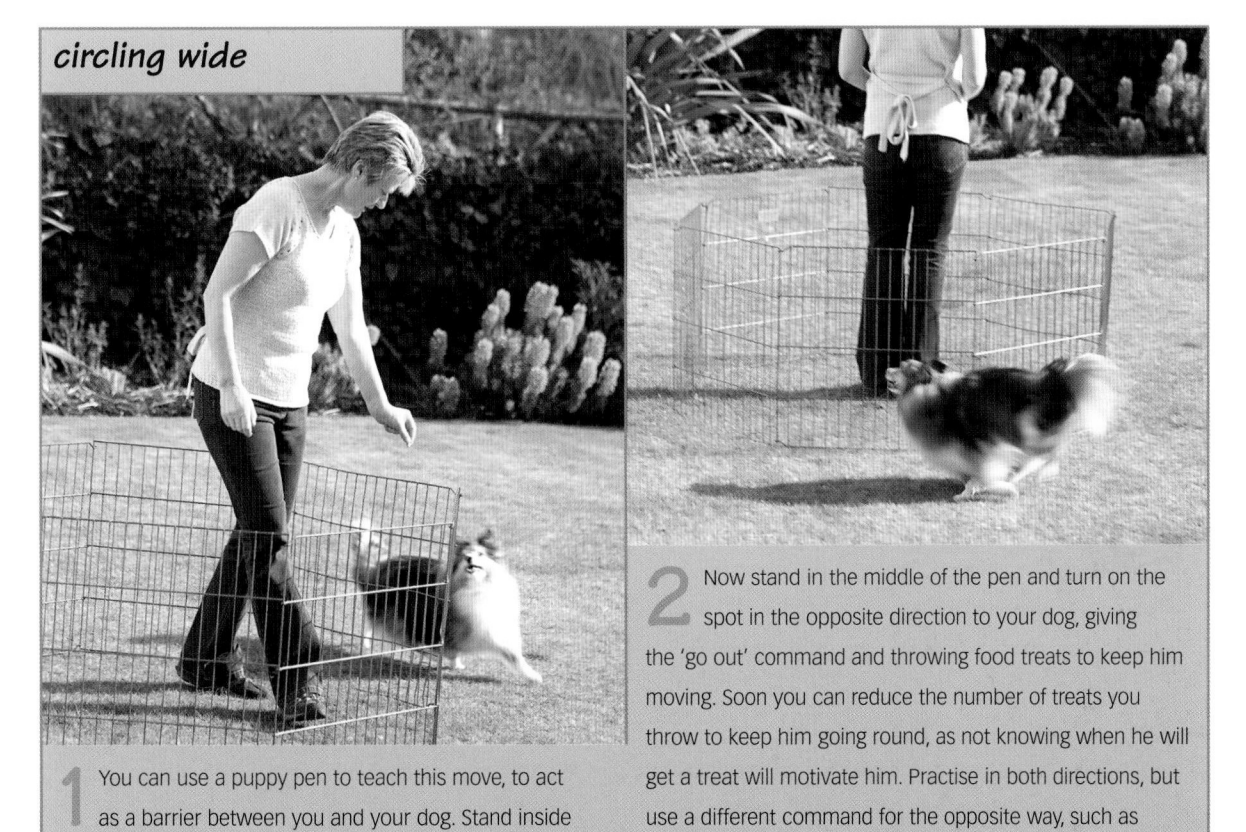

1 You can use a puppy pen to teach this move, to act as a barrier between you and your dog. Stand inside the pen and use a treat to lure him around the outer circumference of the pen. As your dog follows, throw some treats out just in front of him. Click as he moves forward to get the treats but just before he reaches them. Repeat several times, then introduce the command 'go out' before you throw the treats and click.

2 Now stand in the middle of the pen and turn on the spot in the opposite direction to your dog, giving the 'go out' command and throwing food treats to keep him moving. Soon you can reduce the number of treats you throw to keep him going round, as not knowing when he will get a treat will motivate him. Practise in both directions, but use a different command for the opposite way, such as 'wide' instead of 'go out'. Finally, try the move without the puppy pen. Give the command again, and as soon as your dog goes out on a circle around you, throw some treats out wide to keep him on a large circle. If you move in a larger circle your dog will also move in a larger circle, as he knows to keep on your outside.

reverse moves

Teaching your dog to move backwards will increase his back-end awareness and make him think about where he is placing his feet. This is particularly important if you want to take part in agility, as your dog has to learn to leave his back feet on the contact points of some of the equipment.

Back away

Your dog can be taught to walk backwards away from you, which is very useful for distance control in obedience and if you want to try heelwork to music. Small dogs often understand the first method better as they have to take more steps to be able to look up and see your face.

method 2

During freetime (see pages 56–57), simply sit in a chair and wait until your dog takes a step back then click and reward. Repeat, then introduce the command 'walk back' and build up the number of steps.

method 1

1 Stand with your feet slightly apart and place a treat between your heels. Let your dog get the treat and click as he steps back to look up at you. Make sure you click for the step rather than the look up. Put down another treat and repeat.

2 Now, as your dog steps backwards, delay clicking for a second. He will probably take another step back – click as soon as he does this and reward him with another treat between your heels. Repeat until your dog is walking back easily, then introduce the command 'walk back'.

In combination

To put the walk back and reverse through moves together, your dog must be able to do a turn. Start with him standing in front and lure him around as if doing a twist. Once he is facing away, click and throw a treat so he doesn't have to do a full circle. You may have to use your other hand to stop him physically from doing a full twist. Introduce the word 'turn', and click and reward when your dog is facing directly away from you.

super tip!

From a distance, it can be helpful to repeat the 'walk back' command a couple of times, because when your dog is reversing towards you he will find it difficult to see where you are unless he turns his head.

reverse through

1 Stand astride your dog and hold a treat to his nose, gently pushing him backwards. Click as he goes back through your legs. Treat in the close or side position to finish. Repeat until he understands, then dispense with the push and introduce the command 'back up'.

2 Stand a step away from your dog, with your legs wide enough for him to reverse through. Give the command and as he reverses click, then treat when he is in the close or side position. Repeat, then tell your dog to wait and walk behind him. Repeat the move, each time moving further away.

props department

A superdog is super confident, and the earlier in life he is introduced to unusual objects such as a skateboard the better. Once he realizes that standing on an object that moves will not hurt him, he will be well placed to tackle advanced activities such as agility or superdog tricks.

Freetime

Freetime gives your dog or puppy the opportunity to show you what he can do, and develop some moves of his own – with or without props. Keep a clicker and treats handy, to encourage him to repeat some of the moves. Think of your clicker as a small camera and be very aware of how accurately you use it. Be vigilant and click as soon as you see something you like.

A skateboard makes a useful prop for freetime sessions.

Props or not?

Puppy With a puppy, freetime without a prop means 'show me what you can do'. Be realistic, though, as he will not have learned very much and won't be able to show you many moves.

When you put down a prop you may be surprised at what your pup does. At first, click for any interaction, to encourage him to explore with his nose, mouth and feet. If your puppy has never gone on, through or inside objects such as a tunnel, or box, now is the time to give him the opportunity.

A skateboard will accustom your puppy to the feeling of movement. If you go on to do agility competitions, he will have no fear of the seesaw as it lowers to the ground. The advantage of letting your puppy explore a skateboard rather than putting him on it is that he will be far less likely to frighten himself when he finds that it moves.

super tip!

During freetime, throw food away from your puppy so that he doesn't become focused on you and learns to use his initiative. This won't encourage him to sniff around for crumbs, as he will work out that he gets another treat more quickly by continuing to offer moves.

Older dog With an older dog, freetime without props is an opportunity to start shaping some of the moves he offers, which is great fun (see box).

Walking back (see pages 54–55) is one of the most common behaviours a dog is likely to offer. When this happens, click, reward and say 'walk back'. He will quickly begin to understand what this means.

shaping

Many new behaviours are modified or shaped in freetime – for example, changing the 'face' command (paw on nose) into 'cross paws'. The 'face' command is more easily taught from the down position, by placing something like a sticky note on your dog's nose. When he wipes it off, click and treat. When my dog wiped his face, I noticed his paw dropped down and crossed over. Next time, I waited until the wipe had finished and then clicked for the crossed paws action. This shaped the original behaviour into something else. Shaping can take longer than showing your dog what to do, but is often very effective.

fetch!

A dog that knows how to retrieve will bring a toy back to you rather than keeping it for himself, and be much more fun for the family to play with. Retrieving is also an essential skill if you want to train your dog for agility or obedience competitions. Some dogs like picking up objects in their mouths but some breeds, such as Shelties, Greyhounds and Whippets, have softer mouths and can be reluctant.

teaching the retrieve

1 When training, choose a dumbbell that is the correct size and comfortable for your dog to hold. Sit in a chair and hold a dumbbell out towards your dog. When he sniffs it, click and treat. Repeat several times.

2 The next time he sniffs it, withhold the click and see what happens. Your dog may open his mouth to take the dumbbell and, if he does, click. Withhold the click for a little longer each time to encourage your dog to keep hold of the dumbbell.

Leave it!

If you have taught your puppy to play tuggie from an early age (see pages 36–37), he will already be familiar with the 'leave it' command. This will help him now to learn to swap his dumbbell for a treat when asked.

To teach the 'leave it' command, use a tuggie toy to play vigorously with your dog and then suddenly stop, saying 'leave it'. If you keep the tuggie still, he will find it less interesting and let go. When this happens, click and treat.

super tip!

• If you train the retrieve while sitting in a chair, you will not have to bend over as much and it will be easier for your dog to keep his head level.
• When you throw the dumbbell, make sure it has landed before you release your dog to fetch it, as a moving dumbbell may encourage him to stop it with his feet.

3 Next, put the dumbbell on the floor and click your dog for sniffing it. Then click if he picks it up. He may drop it when he hears the click but still reward. Now hold out your hand to see whether he will put the dumbbell in it. If he drops it on the floor and misses your hand, wait to see if he picks it up again. If he successfully puts the dumbbell in your hand, click and reward. Repeat and gradually place the dumbbell further away from you.

4 To get a sit as your dog presents the dumbbell to you, simply hold your hand higher. As he sits, click, but if he drops the dumbbell or misses your hand, don't click again. Wait patiently for him to pick it up and put it in your hand before you reward him. This will teach your dog to hold the dumbbell through the click. Now try the same exercise with you standing up.

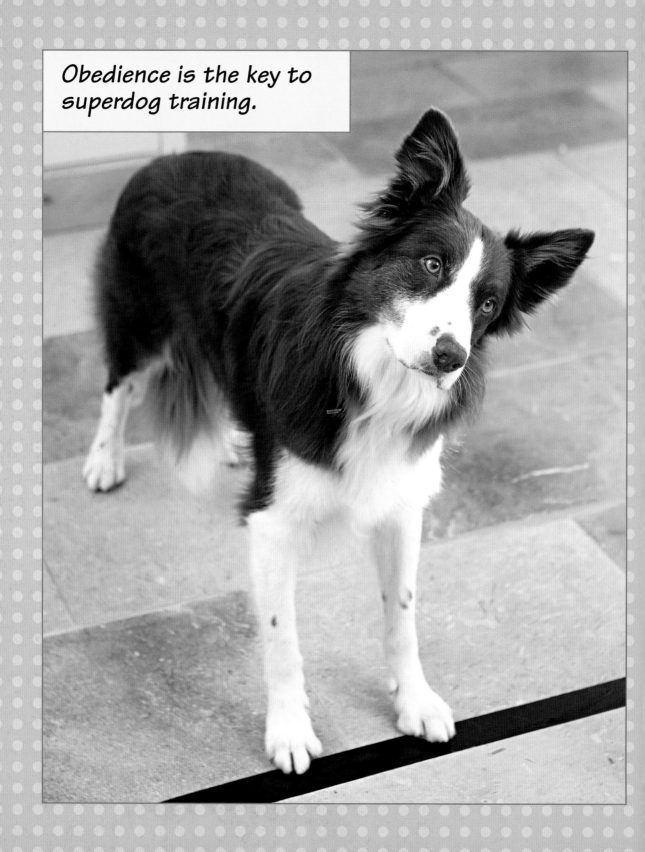

Obedience is the key to superdog training.

SUPERDOG OBEDIENCE

An obedient dog is a joy to live with and to take out and about. You can rely on him to behave well, be respectful and safe, and still have plenty of personality. Such a dog will do as he is asked first time, and although training to this standard can take many months it is a fun process and very worthwhile. It also gives you the opportunity to meet many other like-minded dog owners.

Moving on up

Many owners of all ages and levels of experience enjoy competing with their dogs in obedience competitions. The stages of competition vary from country to country, but there is usually the equivalent of a pre-beginner class followed by novice, then Class A, B, C and Championship C, which require progressively more advanced training.

If you want to compete with your dog, remember that the rules for obedience will vary throughout the world, so before you start make sure you obtain an up-to-date copy of the judges' guidelines from the governing body of your national kennel club.

To compete in the more advanced classes, the exercises your dog will need to learn include:

- Heelwork at different paces.
- Sit, down and stand positions.
- Send away, drop and recall (the dog is sent in a direction as requested by the judge, dropped down on command and then returned to the handler's heelwork position).
- Retrieve a dumbbell or an article provided by the judge.
- Distance control (the dog sits, stands and downs several paces from the handler).
- Sit and down (stays out of sight of the handler).
- Scent discrimination (the dog selects a scented cloth or wooden block).

In various countries, there may be some additional exercises, such as retrieve over a hurdle, drop on recall, redirected send away, redirected retrieve, and scent on leather and metal.

A dog's sense of smell is much stronger than ours.

spot the difference

During a heelwork competition, the dog is required to walk with his handler both on and off the lead, varying according to which class he is competing in. In the more advanced classes, all heelwork is done off the lead (known as heel free) and there will be changes of pace. Rules and requirements vary around the world.

The exercises

In Europe, the heelwork exercises are tested at normal, slow and fast pace speeds, together with turns, turnabouts and halts. The stand, sit and down are performed at a march around an 8 x 8 m (26 x 26 ft) square of cones, anti-clockwise so that left turns are taken at the corners. In the UK, these positions can be done at any time during normal pace heelwork, as directed by the judge.

In several countries, including the USA and Australia, the figure of eight is also part of the heelwork exercise. The US rules currently state: 'The principal feature of this exercise is the ability of the dog and the handler to work as a team. For the figure of eight the handler will stand and the dog will sit in the heel position facing the judge, midway between the two stewards who will be standing 2.5 m (8 ft) apart. The figure of eight in the novice classes will be done on a leash.'

See pages 44–45 for training information on how to teach your dog to walk in the heelwork position. This is vital for everyday control as well as competitions.

From left to right: slow pace with dog walking, normal pace with dog trotting and fast pace, with dog in extended trot.

Hold your arms high to avoid contact with your dog's head.

Arm positions

European rules state that for heelwork the handler's arms must move in a natural position, although in reality there is nothing very natural about how a dog handler holds their arms or the way the dog walks next to his handler. For example, with the 'watch' command, a dog would not normally walk along watching his handler as he does during a competition.

It would not be practical for a dog handler in competition to walk with their hands hanging down by their sides as they would knock against the dog's head. To avoid this, the handler must hold their arms higher or wider, but this is no more natural than the way handlers work with their dogs in the UK, where the left hand is held up against the body, away from the dog's head. The rules state that the dog should work in a natural and happy manner – maybe it is time for the word natural to be taken out, as it is far more important for him to be happy!

distance control

An important element of any obedience test is the handler's ability to control their dog from a distance. The handler must walk away from their dog and then command a total of six positions, which include the sit, down and stand, as directed by the judge. It is also wonderful to have this level of obedience from your superdog at all times, both in the home and when out and about.

Don't move!

With distance control in competition, penalties are incurred if the dog moves away from the set-up line. When training, it is therefore advisable to lure each position in the way that you need your dog to learn it. For example, if the dog is allowed to move no further than a body length in any direction from the set-up line he may be set up with his front paws on the line or mark, which will allow much more versatility in how you teach each position.

In the UK

In the UK the set-up position can be from the down, stand or sit and the dog is required to change position six times at the judge's discretion.

From down

Sit from down Dog's front paws move up into the sit.
Stand from down Dog's paws remain planted and the body rises.

From stand

Sit from stand Dog brings his back legs to his front paws.
Down from stand Dog's front paws remain planted on the line as he moves his rear end back.

In the UK the dog's front paws are set-up on the set up line.

From sit

Stand from sit Dog keeps his front paws still and moves his back legs into the stand.

Down from sit Dog's front paws move forward into the down.

In Europe

The Fédération Cynologique Internationale (FCI) is a worldwide affiliation of kennel clubs. Under FCI rules, the distance control exercise begins and ends with the dog in the down position. To avoid penalties for movement, it is best to set up the dog with his back legs on the set-up line.

From down

Sit from down Dog's front paws move up into the sit.
Stand from down Dog's paws remain planted and the body rises.

From sit

Stand from sit Dog keeps his back paws on the line and moves his front paws forward.

Down from sit Dog's front paws move forward into the down.

signal exercise

In the USA, distance control is referred to as a 'signal exercise'. The handler must heel their dog to one end of the ring, and then stand him and walk away. They must then signal the dog to do a down, sit and come to them. Marks are deducted if the dog walks forward.

From stand

Sit from stand Dog's front paws move back as he sits but his back feet remain in place on the line.

Down from stand Dog's front paws remain planted as he cantilevers back.

Distance training

Lure each position until your dog understands how to do it from a verbal command or hand signal. You can then gradually move further away from him, moving in closer and starting again if you encounter any problems. If your dog walks towards you, use the 'walk back' command (see pages 54–55) to help counter this.

In Europe the dog's back paws should remain on the set-up line to avoid incurring penalties for movement.

scent discrimination

In obedience, 'scent and retrieve' tests a dog's ability to pick out a marked article, pick it up and present it to his handler without chewing or mouthing it, as well as the willingness and speed with which he works. Even if you don't want to compete, you can use scent and retrieve to develop superdog tricks (see pages 68–69).

Hot and cold

Scents are often referred to as 'hot' and 'cold', which simply means scented or not scented. Scenting is done on different objects throughout the world, but here we concentrate on scenting cloths and wood (see pages 68–69).

Store 'cold' cloths carefully in a sealable bag. Washing, steam ironing and freezing will remove (or 'kill') a scent. Always handle clean or 'cold' cloths with a pair of tongs or gloves.

Scent and retrieve on cloth

A series of 'clean' or 'cold' cloths (usually between six and 10) are put down in a pattern with one 'hot' or scented cloth. The dog will then sniff the cloths and pick out the scented one.

In the beginner classes the cloths are set out in a straight line, but in more advanced classes the judge will decide on the arrangement of the cloths, and decoy scents are also used.

Make finding scents fun by hiding your dog's toy behind irretrievable objects.

Place a ceramic tile in the cloth pockets you don't want want your dog to retrieve.

that hold ceramic tiles – to make a pocket, simply fold a cotton cloth in half and sew up the two long sides. The only loose cloth I then put down is the one I want the dog to retrieve.

As a dog will always sniff before he eats anything, I put a food treat on each cloth to maintain his interest and encourage him to bring his nose down and sniff. He will then eat the treats as he works his way across the pattern of cloths.

Relatively inexperienced dogs will eat all the food treats first and then return to pick up the correct cloth. In contrast, an experienced superdog will stop sniffing when he finds the right cloth, then pick it up carefully and return it to you. At this stage it's not always necessary to use food treats, although it can still be useful to put a treat on the first cloth as this will help bring your dog's nose down at the start of the pattern.

Early learning

You can begin teaching scent discrimination to your puppy by throwing a toy into the long grass and encouraging him to sniff it out. This will accustom him to using his nose to find things.

Next hide a toy among a series of heavy articles that your puppy (or beginner dog) can't pick up – such as heavy buckets, stones or bricks. Tell him to 'find' it and bring it to you, clicking and rewarding when he does this successfully.

When your dog is using his nose confidently you can introduce a loose cloth, clicking either as he picks it up or when he presents it to you. Vary the moment of the click, so that your dog doesn't become reliant on it.

Encourage sniffing

A dog can also use his mouth as a way of scenting, but this should be discouraged. To this end, I use cloth pockets

When the dog understands, gradually progress to using only loose cloths.

advanced scenting

Dogs competing in advanced classes must pick out a cloth marked with the judge's scent rather than the handler's. They will scent two cloths: one for the pattern and one for the handler to use to give the dog the scent. The dog must know how to take the scent from the cloth, otherwise he won't be able to discriminate between the judge's scent and the decoys.

taking the scent

Place a treat in your hand and cover it with a cloth. Hold your hand out towards your dog, and when he sniffs the cloth flick it back and allow him to take the treat.

holding the cloth

Your dog should take a very small area of the cloth between his teeth. This will encourage him to do a quicker pick-up than if he grabs a large mouthful of fabric, which will also draw the saliva from his tongue and encourage him to mouth. Teach your dog to take a cloth correctly by only ever holding out a small section towards him. Click for him holding it correctly and reward when you take it from him.

Scent and retrieve with wood

Picking out a scented wooden block is an even more impressive accomplishment for your superdog. In competition, a small wooden block is scented by the handler holding it and then placed among a number of others for the dog to find and retrieve. Points are lost if the dog drops or chews the block, so spend time teaching your dog to hold the block carefully.

Tricky business

Once your dog understands how to perform a scent and retrieve exercise, you can develop this into an impressive party trick, by asking him to retrieve a coloured object of your choice. What your spectators don't have to know is that your dog is not actually picking out a colour, but a smell.

Behind the scenes, place some children's coloured wooden bricks or something similar in a bag, being careful to handle them with tongs rather than your hands so they are not scented. With your dog in a sit, tip out the bricks and pick up the one you want him to find with your hand, then put it back down and tell your friends you will send him to fetch it. Your dog will sniff out the only brick with a 'hot' scent and bring it to you.

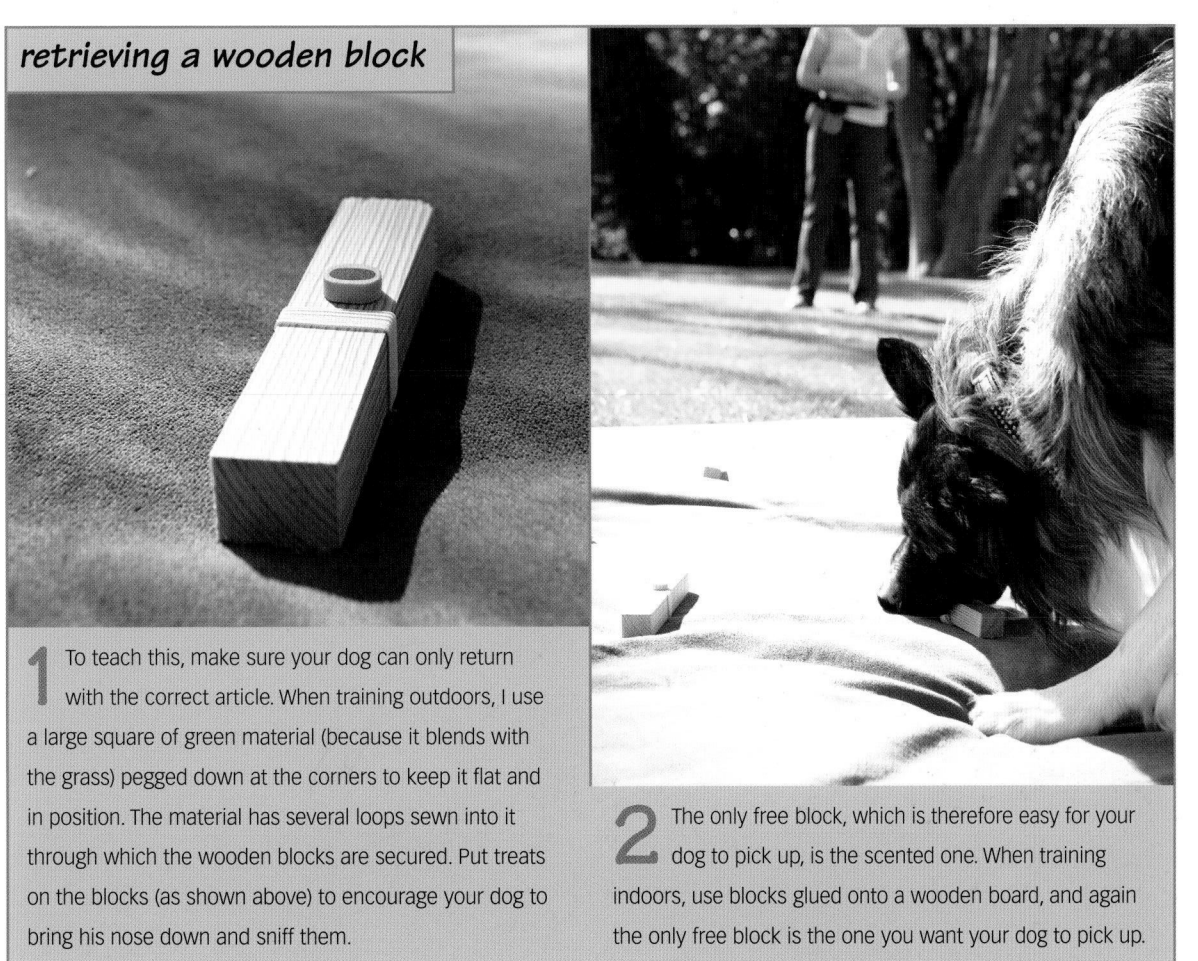

retrieving a wooden block

1 To teach this, make sure your dog can only return with the correct article. When training outdoors, I use a large square of green material (because it blends with the grass) pegged down at the corners to keep it flat and in position. The material has several loops sewn into it through which the wooden blocks are secured. Put treats on the blocks (as shown above) to encourage your dog to bring his nose down and sniff them.

2 The only free block, which is therefore easy for your dog to pick up, is the scented one. When training indoors, use blocks glued onto a wooden board, and again the only free block is the one you want your dog to pick up.

sending away

This exercise is an impressive demonstration of your distance control and your superdog's abilities. Even if you don't want to compete, having such control can be extremely useful. For example, if you have a nervous visitor you can send your dog to his bed, which will be very reassuring.

Send away, drop and recall

The handler is required to send the dog away to a place specified by the judge. The dog is dropped down and then recalled to the handler, walking at heel until told to stop. In some countries the dog is sent away to a box of four markers, and in the advanced classes he may be sent to a cone and redirected to a box, which may be to the right or left.

teaching the send away

1 First, your dog should be able to go to a target and down (see pages 34–35). Place a target mat at the back of a marker or in the middle of a box of cones, and click and reward your dog as he goes down on the mat. Then put a sending command, such as 'go' or 'away', to the move and click him for downing on the mat. Whenever your dog sees that particular target mat, he will now know he must drop down on it.

2 Next, your dog should stay in the down until released. Stay close to the mat and, as he drops down, click and reward. If he gets up after the click, put him down again but don't click, just reward.

Redirected send away

The redirected send away is a European obedience exercise for true superdogs. The dog is sent to a cone using verbal commands and/or arm signals, then after a few seconds is redirected to a square approximately 25 m (82 ft) away and drops down on command. The handler walks towards the dog and turns away again, before calling him and walking back to the start.

sending to the cone

Begin by teaching your dog to run around a cone and back to you. Click as he rounds the cone and reward when he reaches you. Now move closer to the cone and send your dog around it, stopping him in a wait as he reaches the other side. When he is opposite you, click and reward. The 'in front' command will help to straighten him and make redirection much easier.

teaching redirection

While your dog is watching, put down a target mat and stand sideways onto it a short distance away, with your dog in front. Send him to the target with an arm signal and verbal command. Repeat on the other side. Now have your dog in position at the cone and redirect him to his mat. Finally, introduce a box of cones around the mat and build up the distance to send him to the cone, and then to the box.

super tip!
Work on both steps together and separately, to avoid your dog anticipating or valuing one element more than the other.

retrieve over a hurdle

This European exercise also forms part of the World Cup competition at Crufts Dog Show, so is worth teaching if you have such ambitions. It's also a fun and energetic game to play at home with your superdog, once he's reached around 12 months of age. In competition, the handler stands about 3 m (10 ft) in front of a hurdle with the dog at heel. They throw a dumbbell over the hurdle, then tell the dog to jump it, retrieve the dumbbell and jump back again.

Training your dog to jump

Start with a low pole to encourage your dog to go over the jump rather than under it. Tell your dog to wait while you step over the jump, then take a couple of strides before turning to face him. Recall him enthusiastically, holding your arms wide, clicking as he jumps and treating when he gets to you. Repeat several times, then introduce the command 'over'.

Once your dog is comfortable with going over the jump, try putting him in a wait and then throw a treat over the jump, giving a release command such as 'OK' for him to get it. Alternatively, place a target such as a small mat or

Teaching your dog to jump over a single pole will produce a better jumping style.

The height of the hurdle should be appropriate for the size of the dog.

super tip!
The further you throw the dumbbell for the retrieve the better. If you only throw it a short distance and it doesn't land straight, your dog may be tempted to come around the jump instead of back over it. Practise throwing a dumbbell until you are able to make it land where you want it to.

plastic lid on the other side of the jump and send your dog over to it, click and recall him to you to get his reward.

High and wide
The hurdle should be 1 m (3 ft) wide and approximately as high as the dog's withers, but never more than 1 m (3 ft) high. Three different sizes and weights of metal dumbbell are available, in proportion to the size of the dog.

Filler fences
Unlike in agility, where the jumps always consist of poles, the jump for retrieve over a hurdle is always a filler fence, making it difficult for the dog to see the dumbbell he must retrieve. Up until now your dog will have jumped only very low poles, so gradually build up the height until it is almost at his withers and then introduce a filler.

Metal dumbbells
Under FCI rules the dumbbell should be metal, which some dogs – particularly those with a soft mouth or sensitive teeth – dislike holding. Help your dog by teaching

him to hold a wide range of articles securely, as any mouthing will make holding a metal dumbbell more uncomfortable. You could also introduce him to a metal dumbbell by putting vet-wrap or something similar around the middle of it. When you give your dog the dumbbell, keep his head level until he learns to hold it properly. If his head is too high the dumbbell can drop back into his mouth, which may encourage mouthing.

Use the size and weight of dumbbell appropriate for your dog.

Superdog agility is fun, fast and furious!

SUPERDOG AGILITY

Agility is an exhilarating sport that tests how well you and your dog work together. Begin by taking your dog for some basic agility training, and if you enjoy it you may wish to try competing in elementary classes, working your way up to more advanced levels.

Competing

An agility competiton is informal and fun but also fast and furious. You must be quick witted and physically fit or have super control of your dog at a distance. You can also find classes for children to attend with their dogs, but even if your child does not want to compete they will enjoy setting up a doggy obstacle course in the garden.

Precision and speed

Agility is all about precision and speed – a superdog can tackle 20 obstacles in under 30 seconds. The courses are complicated enough to make it impossible for a dog to go round by himself without direction from his handler, so it is up to you to remember the course. Walking it properly beforehand, committing it to memory and developing a strategy for tackling the obstacles in the fastest way possible are all vital to success.

Classes

Provided a dog is fit, agility is suitable for all kinds of breeds. Classes are divided by height into small, medium and large according to measurements given by the sport's governing body, such as the American Kennel Club (AKC) in the USA, the FCI in Europe and the Kennel Club in the UK. Measurements are taken up to the dog's withers and courses adjusted accordingly.

An agility arena measures about 32 x 32 m (100 x 100 ft) and will include a variety of obstacles such as jumps, weaving poles, tunnels, tyres, a seesaw (known as a teeter-totter in the USA), dog walk and A-frame. There are also jumping classes that omit contact equipment.

Agility breeds

Among the large breeds, the most competitive dogs are Border Collie, Kelpie and Belgian Shepherd, as well as various crossbreeds. In the UK, there is also a large dog competition called ABC (Anything But a Collie) to showcase other breeds in a final of their own. Successful smaller breeds include Poodles, Shetland Sheepdogs and Terriers.

A superdog can complete an agility course at an impressive speed.

training for agility

To be an agility superdog, your dog needs a thorough grounding in basic obedience training. He must understand the send away and do a good wait. Agility dogs can become strong and very motivated when running a course and tend to pick their own line, so you need to have good control to bring your dog back to the heel and side positions. A superdog is highly aware of how to use his legs and back end to get into position as quickly as possible.

Play and reward

To encourage the enthusiasm and high energy needed in agility, keep some high-value toys to use as rewards. This is one reason it is important for your dog to play tuggie (see pages 36–37), as food rewards may not provide the necessary motivation.

The wait

The wait (see pages 42–43) is extremely important, as your dog must wait on the start line before you call him. Ideally, you should only need to give the 'wait' command once for him to obey. This way, your dog will know that the next time you call him it will be to start the course, so he will

A game of tuggie can be used as a reward, to encourage motivation and enthusiasm.

not get into the habit of anticipating. The call command should always be given *before* you move, so that your dog cannot read your body language.

Breaking the wait

An over-enthusiastic dog may break his wait at the start. If this happens during training, don't be tempted to handle your dog – he may see this as a reward and be encouraged to break the wait again in the future. Instead, go back to working on improving his understanding of the heel and side positions (see pages 44–45), so that he knows exactly where to go without having to be pulled or pushed into position. After that, practise by putting your dog into a wait, then click, return and reward.

Join the club

Very few handlers are lucky enough to have a full set of agility equipment at home, so it is a good idea to join a specialist club. You can find details of these via your local kennel club, the internet or the notice board at your veterinary surgery.

Your dog will benefit from working with other dogs, and learn to ignore the new scents and distractions he will

super tip!
Every rule is made to be broken, and a dog that is habitually slow to come off the start line may benefit from being given the 'wait' command several times, so that he is encouraged to anticipate.

encounter. This will be a huge advantage when you eventually enter a competition.

You will be able to use the club's equipment and learn from an experienced agility trainer, as well as get advice from other handlers. If there are indoor facilities with a good non-slip surface this can be invaluable in bad weather or during the winter months, when poor light makes outdoor training difficult.

Find a friend

Having a training partner who is willing to help you, perhaps by holding or calling your dog when he first learns to negotiate a new piece of equipment, can be extremely beneficial in agility.

Two people are always better than one to help with agility training.

groundwork for jumping

All you really need to teach the groundwork for jumping is a single pair of jump wings (wood or plastic structures that support jump poles). You can teach your superdog to go through them, send away, recall, and work in circles and figures of eight around them. All these are vital for agility and will help to make your dog supple and obedient.

Body language

When teaching the following exercises, it is very important that your body language always gives your dog the correct signals. For example, your body must face in the direction in which you want him to go, and your signalling arm should always be the one that is nearest to the dog. You can begin to introduce right and left verbal commands at this stage of his training.

turning left and right

Set up a pair of wings and, with your dog on your left, keep him in position as you both turn to the right around a wing. Then practise turning left with your dog on your right. These turns are fairly easy for him as you are both moving in the same direction.

recall and send away through wings

Begin with just one pair of wings. Put your dog in a wait, then recall him through. Build up the recall, so that eventually he will go through three pairs of wings to reach you. Now send your dog away to a target or toy. Begin with one pair of wings and gradually build up the send away until he will go through several pairs.

figure of eight

1 Send your dog away on a left turn around a wing. Your body should face to the left. As your dog wraps around the wing, move your body, arms and legs clockwise to the right in a smooth movement – but do not move before your dog is committed to going around the wing, or he may go back.

2 Continue moving your body in a figure of eight, which your dog's movement mirrors as he turns right around the other wing and sets off to start the move again.

changing behind

1 Valuable time can be saved by changing direction behind your dog while he negotiates an obstacle. This means he must turn away from you, which is more difficult as he is used to following your body movement. Stand next to a jump wing with your dog on your left, between you and the wing. Using your left hand signal and verbal command, send him around the wing in a small left circle, similar to the twist on pages 50–51. Repeat on both sides. Practise until your dog can do more than one circle and the movements are fast and fluid.

2 Now progress to moving towards the wing together. As you move, give your dog the left command and see if he turns away from you. If not, continue practising from a standstill before trying again. When your dog is old enough to jump (around 12 months) practise the same exercise over a low pole, gradually increasing the height.

jumping in agility

The groundwork you did to prepare your dog for jumping (see pages 78–79) will have helped give you the control to direct him in an agility competition. Now is the time to introduce some height to his jumping.

Teaching your dog to jump

Start with a low pole to encourage your dog to go over it and make a nice shape. You want him to take off with his front feet and land with his front feet, rather than taking off and landing on all four feet as this will slow him down. See pages 72–73 for more advice on jump training.

Practise incorporating all the groundwork exercises your dog has learned into his jump training. If your dog goes under the jump it is because you have gone up in height too soon, so lower the pole and start again. If he seems reluctant to jump he may have lost confidence, so again lower the pole and encourage him with treats and toys.

Superdog jumping

A superdog needs accuracy and speed when jumping a course. It is no good trying to work with a really crazy fast

Your dog should land with his front feet first.

dog, but if you do your groundwork properly it will help when you start running together. A slower dog can be made faster with hard work and lots of motivation, but to really succeed in agility a dog has to be super fast and possess natural acceleration.

Missing a jump

What you should do if your dog misses a jump will depend on whether he is naturally fast or slow. I have found that opposites usually work. For example: **With a fast dog**, if he does, say, three jumps out of a line of four and then goes across your body and misses out the fourth, don't turn in a circle to get him back as this will not break his flow. Simply stand still and bring him back to the side on which he was working, before sending him on over the fourth jump. **With a slow dog,** it might be better to turn a circle to maintain the flow rather than bringing him back into position.

super tip!

In agility, if your dog is on your left side to do an exercise he should stay there until told otherwise. If he breaks position, bring him back into the heel position before continuing. The same applies to the right side. For arm signals, use the arm nearest your dog so that your body language is clear, and consistently in the direction in which you are travelling.

Faults

There are different kinds of jump in agility including a hurdle, rising spread jump (two single jumps placed together), hoop (or tyre) and long jump. The dog is penalized five points if he knocks down a jump pole or refuses an obstacle. Three refusals results in elimination.

Only increase jumps to competition height once your dog has developed a good technique.

contact points

Contact obstacles include the A-frame, dog walk and seesaw (teeter-totter). These pieces of equipment are painted in a solid colour, with the contact point or zone at each end in a contrasting colour to indicate where your dog's paws are expected to make contact. The aim is to get him to run as fast as he can across the equipment. Penalties are incurred if he fails to make contact at either end.

Walk the plank

Begin by putting a plank of wood on the ground and, with your dog on the lead, encourage him to walk on it. You can even do this with a young puppy as it will not do him any harm. Click and reward for your dog putting one foot on the plank, then two, and so on. Continue until your dog will happily walk along the plank on either side of you.

target training contact

1 Once your dog is moving confidently along the plank, introduce a target on the ground at the end. Use something that is not highly visible, such as a clear plastic lid, and put a treat on it. Your dog is able to discriminate between the plank and the ground; by placing a target just far enough away from the plank you can encourage him to have his back feet on the plank and front feet off – making the contact and targeting the lid at the same time. The lead will help you to control your dog in the stop position. Then click and make him wait for the reward.

2 A superdog must always be aware of what his back legs are doing. Most dogs are more naturally balanced to the right and are more comfortable to your left. To help counter this, practise walking and running him up and down the plank equally on both sides. Then remove the lead and practise until your dog is happy to run quickly along the plank and targets the lid without a treat on it. Click and reward, always using the hand nearest your dog to keep his head straight.

3 Do not raise the equipment to its full height until your dog is 12 months old.

balancing acts

The A-frame consists of two platforms, usually about 1 m (3 ft) wide and 3 m (10 ft) long, raised up from the ground into an 'A' shape. Most have narrow slats along their length, to make it easier for the dog to secure a grip as he makes his ascent and descent. The seesaw (teeter-totter) is a long plank that pivots in the middle. The more confident your dog is about walking on things that move (see pages 56–57), the better he will be at tackling this. It is difficult to improvise an A-frame or seesaw successfully, and if you want to compete it is worth using the correct equipment.

A-frame

The A-frame is trained in the same way as the dog walk (see pages 82–83) but is a more challenging piece of equipment as it is steeper. To counter this, always start training with the frame at its lowest level to maintain your dog's confidence. The aim is for him to go up and over the frame as fast as possible, making the contact at both ends.

Making contact

Some dogs will make a natural running contact without ever wanting to jump off the A-frame, while small dogs often take the contact in their natural stride so you may never have to train them. To check if this is the case with your dog, try running him across the frame and watching closely – there may be no need for you to teach him the

A dog should be at least 12 months old before tackling an A frame at full height.

An experienced dog will offer the behaviour without a target.

target method described on pages 82–83. However, remember that you must be physically fit and capable of keeping up with your dog as he makes the contact in order to be in the right position for the next obstacle on the course.

Seesaw (teeter-totter)

The movement and noise of a seesaw can frighten a dog, so prepare yours by accustoming him to playing on moving objects (see pages 56–57). The aim is for your dog to ascend and descend the seesaw quickly, but he must touch the contact point with the plank on the ground before alighting.

super tip!

There is a point of tip on the seesaw and it is best to encourage your dog to go past this without hesitation. The seesaw will fall to the ground more quickly, thereby saving a second or two, but your dog will need confidence to do this.

how to make contact

1 If you have a small dog, you will need a helper so you can encourage your dog while they control the seesaw. First squash a treat high onto the contact point. As your dog stops to eat, click and have your helper simultaneously lower the seesaw to the ground.

2 Also put a target on the ground. As the seesaw lowers, click when your dog touches the target, so his back feet remain on the contact point. Big dogs will tip the seesaw earlier, so squash a treat nearer the pivot point.

weaving

Weaving through a set of poles is considered the most challenging of all agility exercises. Your dog must be able to enter the poles correctly and weave in and out at speed, without missing out any of them as he works his way through.

Rhythm

If you watch dogs when they are weaving you will notice that there are two distinct styles. Some adopt a two-footed bounce and others prefer a one-footed rhythm. The style that a dog uses often depends on how he was originally taught to negotiate the weaving poles. Usually a one-footed rhythm will produce a faster time in competition.

Training methods

When training your dog you can use an upright, channel or V-weave, but once the poles are completely upright and in position as for competition the final result will be the same. Although the channel and V-weave methods take longer to teach, they will normally produce a faster weave. The upright weave is the quickest method of training your

These pictures clearly show the two-footed bounce and one-footed rhythm style weaving.

dog, but he may ultimately not be as fast going through. All these methods are explained in detail on pages 88–89).

Upright weave
The dog is taught to go through weave poles in the upright position by luring him in and out with a hand target or target stick. This will usually result in him adopting a two-footed bounce in and out of the poles.

Channel method
This enables the dog to move with greater speed in the beginning and will also encourage the fast one-footed rhythm in and out of the poles. Most small breeds have difficulty with this style because of the width of the poles. When teaching the channel method, it is quicker to work with a helper who can hold the dog or call him through the channel.

V-weave
The weave poles are set in a wide 'V' to start with and then gradually straightened during training, until they are completely upright. This method will usually result in the dog adopting a one-footed rhythm in and out of the poles.

Making an entrance
Your dog must always enter the poles with the pole at his left shoulder. It is a good idea to teach the entry into the weave using two separate poles, so that when any of the training methods is in the final stage, with the poles upright, your dog knows how to enter them correctly. Do this by putting two poles into the ground and clicking your dog for going through the poles with the pole at his left shoulder.

Practise sending your dog through the poles from different angles. It is always easier for him to pick up the entry from an angle off to the left of the line of poles, as he has a pole to wrap around. It is harder for him to pick up an entry from the right because he must go between two poles. Putting up two poles makes it easier as there is only one available gap for your dog to run through.

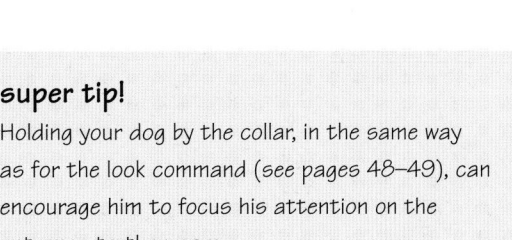

Use two separate poles to teach your dog the correct entry method.

super tip!
Holding your dog by the collar, in the same way as for the look command (see pages 48–49), can encourage him to focus his attention on the entrance to the weave.

superdog weaving

You can buy channel and V-weaves on frames, which will make training easier, but you can also use stick-in-the-ground poles. These are easier to store and less expensive, but have to be repositioned constantly while training.

teaching upright weave

Place the poles in the upright, finished position and simply lure your dog through using a hand target or target stick, keeping his head as level as possible so that he can see the poles. If your dog's head is too low he will look at his feet and never develop the correct weaving style. When luring, don't take your arm or stick out too far from the poles or you will create too big a bounce. Introduce the 'weave' command as your dog is going through the poles.

teaching channel weave

1 Set up 12 poles, 51 cm (21 in) apart, in a straight line and move every other pole 45 cm (18 in) to the right to form a parallel channel. Either end may be used as the start. Clip-on plastic guides can be attached to keep your dog inside the channel. Put a target at the end of the channel, give the target command and click your dog for running through to it.

2 Gradually reduce the width between the poles until they are in line with each other, and introduce the 'weave' command as your dog is weaving through the poles. You can also work on his angled entry into the poles (see pages 86–87) when the plastic guides are on.

Perfect timing

Your dog will move at speed into the weave, and must learn to use his back end as a brake in order to get into the narrow gap and weave fast through the poles. If the timing goes awry and your dog misses out a pole, stand still and get him back to the side on which he was working, then carry on.

Handlers often make the mistake of turning a circle to the start with their dog but this can aggravate the problem rather than remedy it.

super tip!

Always try to correct a problem at the point it occurred. For example, if there are 12 poles and your dog comes out at number 10, by going back to the beginning to start again you can inadvertently train him to keep coming out at the 10th pole. However, by standing still and making your dog do the last two poles you correct the problem where things went wrong.

teaching v-weave

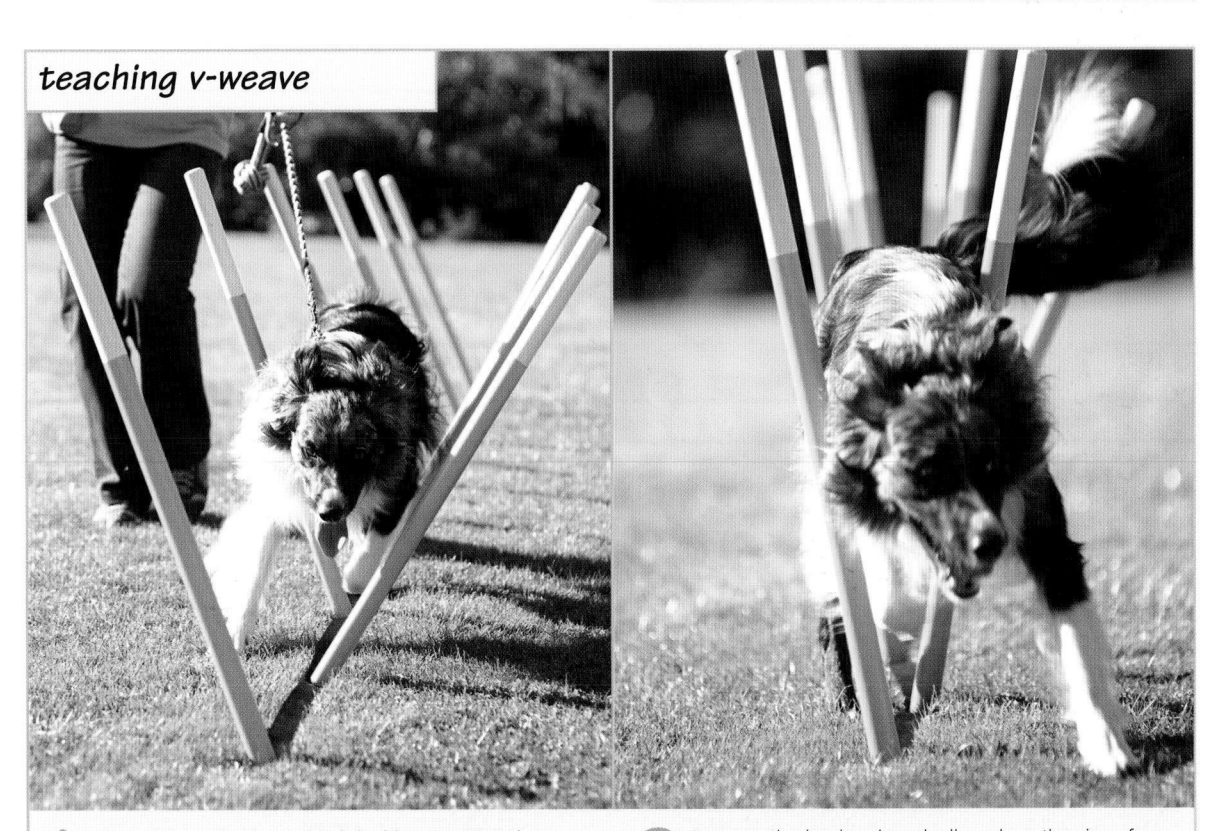

1 Arrange the poles in a wide 'V' with a target at the end. Put your dog on a lead and allow him to pull you through to get to his target and reward. Repeat several times, giving the 'weave' command as he goes through.

2 Remove the lead and gradually reduce the size of the V until the poles are upright. If you encounter any problems, go back to the previous stage.

tunnel vision

Tunnels are relatively simple agility obstacles for a dog to negotiate. Most can be encouraged to go through fairly easily, but this is another exercise where in the initial stages it is very useful to enlist a helper to hold your dog at the tunnel entrance while you call him through, and be ready to reward him with treats or a toy.

Tunnel design

There are two types of tunnel: a collapsible design that is made from non-rigid material, and a rigid pipe version that can be bent into different shapes. These are available from specialist agility equipment suppliers, or via the internet. Always teach the pipe tunnel first as this is easier for your dog to negotiate.

pipe tunnel

1 Squeeze the tunnel up to its shortest length. Put your dog in a sit or down position as close to the tunnel entrance as possible and if necessary ask your helper to hold his collar. Now crouch down at the other end and call your dog through.

2 Encourage your dog into the tunnel and click as he comes, throwing a toy as he gets to you or rewarding him generously with treats. Gradually extend the length of the tunnel and introduce a verbal command, such as 'tunnel'. You can also start to put a bend in the tunnel. Eventually you should be able to run with your dog and send him through the tunnel with just the verbal command. Practise entering the tunnel from both right and left sides.

collapsible tunnel

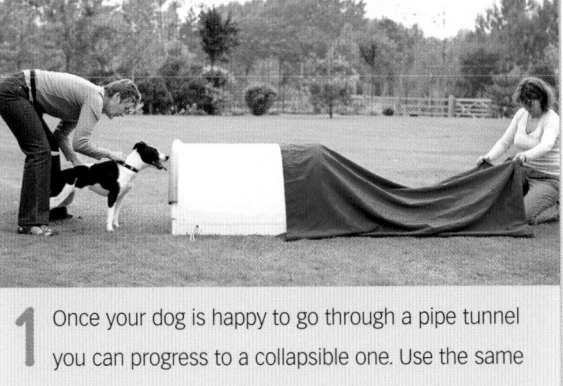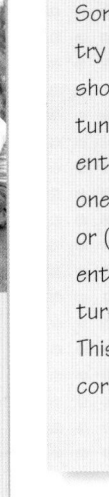

1 Once your dog is happy to go through a pipe tunnel you can progress to a collapsible one. Use the same method, shortening the tunnel by folding the cloth back.

super tip!

Some dogs enjoy tunnels so much that they will try to shoot through whenever they see one, which should not be encouraged. In competition the tunnel is often curved around, showing both entrances to your dog. You could physically block one of the entrances to ensure he doesn't use it, or (if you are confident) run past the wrong entrance, keeping your dog near your leg, and then turn him away from you into the correct entrance. This move is a half twist (see pages 50–51). Done correctly, it can save valuable time.

2 Ask your helper to hold up the tunnel until your dog becomes accustomed to pushing his way through. As your dog begins to understand what he is expected to do, gradually extend the tunnel to its full length.

3 Your helper should gradually lower the cloth onto your dog's back before you try asking him to push his own way through. Click as he is going through and throw a toy or food reward as he bursts through the end.

jumping through a tyre

The 'look' command (see pages 48–49) is vital in teaching your dog to jump through a tyre. Unlike a pole jump, where your dog can literally throw himself over at the last moment, now he must look and judge the aperture carefully to negotiate the tyre safely. Always start with the tyre low and gradually raise it up to maintain confidence.

Tyre designs

In Europe and the USA, the agility tyre jump consists of a tyre suspended on chains, while in the UK it is bolted directly onto two uprights. The tyre can also be a lifebuoy, or a soft fabric hoop to reduce the risk of injury. Any tyre jump must be secure so that your dog cannot knock it over.

teaching the tyre jump

1 Lower the tyre as far as possible, then position your dog in front of it and put him into a sit. Tell him to wait and walk to the other side of the tyre. Kneel down so your dog can see you and give the recall command. Click as he jumps through and reward when he gets to you. Repeat several times, then introduce a command such as 'tyre'. It is important that your dog looks forward at the tyre to judge where the centre is. Hold him by the collar and give the 'tyre, look' command.

2 Throw a toy through the tyre and send your dog through to get it. Gradually raise the tyre height until it is at competition height for the size of your dog.

3 Now practise running together, making sure he looks forward to take the tyre. Practise on both sides.

Long jump

Referred to in some countries as a broad jump, a long jump consists of three to five units with a marker post at each outer corner, which helps the judge to see that a dog has passed correctly from front to back. A dog has to jump reasonably high in order to get the length of the jump, which varies for small, medium and large dogs.

teaching the long jump

1 Start with your dog in a stand or sit in front of two or three elements. These should have some space between them so that he is not encouraged to stand on the units. Put the smallest element on top of the front element to add more height, making it easier for him to clear the jump when it is lengthened. Give the 'wait' command and move to the other end of the long jump. Pause before recalling your dog so that he doesn't learn to anticipate the move.

2 Click as he jumps over and reward when he gets to you. Gradually increase the length of the jump and introduce a different command such as 'right over'. Practise running with your dog and giving the 'right over' command on both sides.

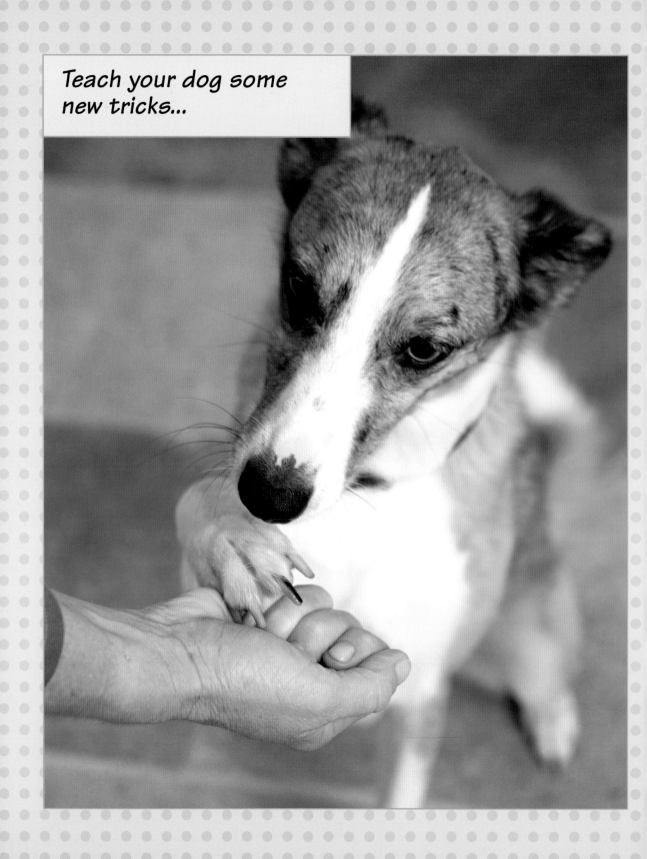

Teach your dog some new tricks...

SUPERDOG PARTY TRICKS

Teaching your dog new tricks can be a very amusing pastime, but they are not purely for entertainment – learning something new is extremely good for your dog, both mentally and physically. A superdog needs to be very aware of his body and leg positions in order to succeed in other disciplines, and the stimulation of learning tricks will help to achieve this. You can start the training when your dog is a young puppy, as at this age he will be particularly flexible and agile.

Benefits of teaching tricks

If you start working with your puppy from an early age, you will begin to develop a bond between you. A superdog is always keen to learn and all the tricks mentioned in this section include moves that a dog would do naturally – you are just teaching him to do them on command, sometimes with props and sometimes without. In fact, the more your dog knows, the easier he will find it to learn new things. This is because he will be much more aware of how his body moves.

Teaching tricks should be a fun experience for both of you. Your dog will enjoy spending quality time with you, and will relish the opportunity to use his brain and work out what you want him to do. His physical fitness will improve, and all the extra praise and treats you give him will be very motivating.

As for you, it is always rewarding to take time out from a busy day and focus on doing something fun with your dog. Teaching him new tricks will help to improve his general level of obedience and make him much more responsive to you. It is also an incredibly rewarding experience to teach your dog something new and discover just how smart your superdog really is.

Teaching an older dog

Even a senior dog can learn new tricks, but take into account his fitness and general health. If in doubt, seek veterinary advice before you begin teaching a new activity.

Use your dog's favourite toys to help him learn.

paw work

Dogs are either right or left handed, although they are more usually right. Watch carefully to see which paw your dog favours naturally, as you can help him learn more easily by starting on his 'easier' side. Then always practise tricks equally on both sides, to help him develop better balance and suppleness.

shake hands

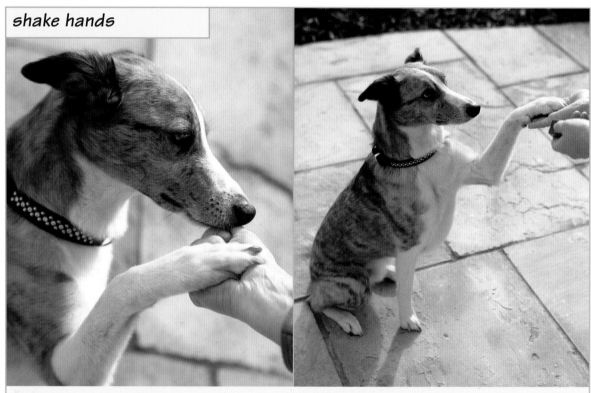

1 Kneel down and put your dog in a sit. Hold out a treat for him to sniff. Position your hand a little to the side to off-balance him slightly as this will shift his weight, making it easier for him to lift a paw. Invite him to get the treat by saying 'get it'. Most dogs will use a paw to try to open your hand. As soon as his paw makes contact, click and reward. Repeat on both sides, then introduce a verbal command for each paw such as 'touch' for the right and 'tap' for the left.

2 Now hold a treat in one hand and open the palm of your other hand towards the leg you want your dog to lift. As soon as his paw touches your palm, click and reward. Repeat on both sides, then gradually move from a kneeling to a standing position.

waving goodbye

Keep repeating the 'touch' (or 'tap') command with your hand slightly out of reach, so that your dog lifts his paw up and lowers it in a waving motion. Click when his paw reaches a more extended position and reward. Repeat, then introduce a 'wave' command after saying 'tap tap' or 'touch touch', until you can use the word 'wave' alone.

On the march

You can also transfer the 'touch' and 'tap' commands from your hand to your leg. Give the paw command and put out your leg at the same time, clicking when your dog touches it. Begin with him in a sit, then progress to him standing in front and finally in the heelwork position, where you can practise marching together.

Lift your left foot and open the palm of your left hand. Your dog should follow the signal to lift his left paw. Repeat on the right paw. Start with just one or two steps, then you can build this into a short marching sequence. Gradually you will be able to dispense with the open hand signal, as your dog will soon associate your raised foot with the paw you want him to lift. Marching together always looks impressive in a heelwork to music routine.

it's a wrap

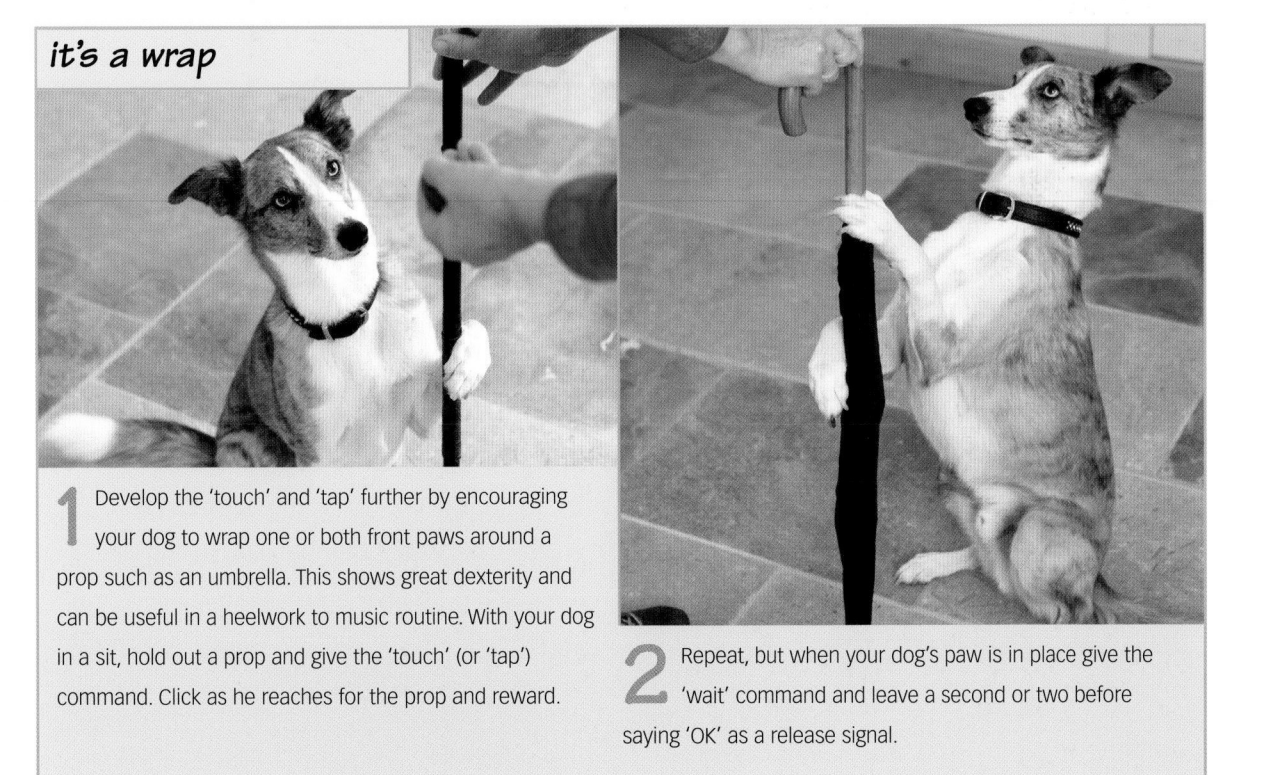

1 Develop the 'touch' and 'tap' further by encouraging your dog to wrap one or both front paws around a prop such as an umbrella. This shows great dexterity and can be useful in a heelwork to music routine. With your dog in a sit, hold out a prop and give the 'touch' (or 'tap') command. Click as he reaches for the prop and reward.

2 Repeat, but when your dog's paw is in place give the 'wait' command and leave a second or two before saying 'OK' as a release signal.

paws for thought

A superdog that gives a 'high five' always looks impressive. You may prefer to teach these moves using a button clicker operated under your foot, as this leaves your hands free to give a visual signal and reward your dog.

More please!

In the beg, your dog learns to sit back and balance on his haunches as he lifts up both front paws. Begin with him in a sit and hold out a treat towards his nose, moving your hand upwards and pushing it away slightly so that your dog's head is tilted backwards. This will off-balance him slightly and bring his paws up off the ground. Click when this happens and reward after his feet drop back to the floor.

Keep practising, and each time ask your dog to lift his paws a little higher until he finds his point of balance. Delay the click for a second or two, and once he can lift both paws and balance comfortably introduce the verbal command 'both' or 'beg'.

high five in a sit

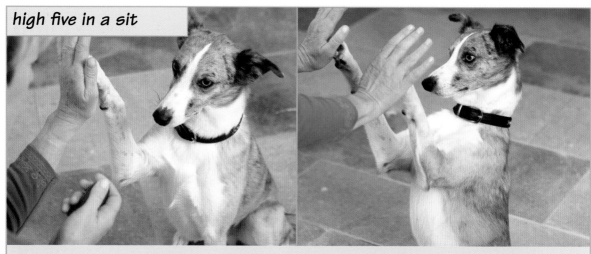

1 Put your dog in a sit, then kneel down as you give the 'touch' (or 'tap') command and hold out your open palm so that he gives a paw (see pages 96–97). Repeat several times. Next, change your hand position to a raised 'high five' and simultaneously give the 'touch' (or 'tap') command. As soon as his paw touches your raised hand, click and reward.

2 Repeat, introducing the 'high five' command as your dog makes contact with your hand. Click and reward. Practise until he will happily touch your hand just from the verbal command. Repeat on both sides. Now stand up and put your dog into a beg, hold out both hands and say 'high five'. Click and reward if he goes to touch both hands. If he has difficulty making contact, move in closer so it is easier for him.

say a prayer

1 There are times when even a superdog needs a little heavenly inspiration and teaching him to lower his head as if in prayer can certainly give this impression! Kneel down and put your dog in a sit. Give the 'touch' (or 'tap') command so that he touches your leg, then give the 'both' (or 'beg') command so that he puts both paws on your leg. Say 'wait' to keep him in position, then click. Now move your treat hand underneath and between his front paws so that he has to lower his head into a 'praying' position to get it. Repeat several times, then introduce the verbal command 'pray'.

2 You can develop variations, such as your dog jumping onto a chair, putting both front paws on the back of it and then bowing his head as if in prayer. Alternatively, you can sit on the chair and hold an arm outstretched for your dog to put his paws on.

tall orders

Some dogs seem to enjoy working on their back legs and it's certainly something many do naturally, perhaps to get a better view from a window or to attract your attention. Small dogs in particular often find standing tall very easy, but others may find it more challenging.

stand tall

1 Depending on the size of your dog, stand or kneel down and hold a treat over his head. Now give the 'both' command, and as he lifts his front legs move the treat up and slightly behind him, so that he pushes up onto his hind legs. Click and reward. Repeat several times until your dog understands that you want him to lift both front paws off the ground.

2 Gradually hold the treat up higher so that your dog lifts up his paws and balances more. With practice, he should be able to balance for a second or two before you click and treat. Some dogs, particularly smaller ones, can find it intimidating if you stand over them when they are on their back legs, so in this case wait until your dog is confident about the move before you stand up and ask for it.

Take care

Don't ask a dog that is less than one year old to try to stand upright on command as this can damage his joints. Be equally careful with an older dog, as he may find it more difficult.

super tip!

Don't worry about confusing your dog with the 'both' command. He will soon understand that when you say the word it means he should lift both front paws off the ground. In a sit this will result in a beg (see pages 98–99) and in a stand he will stand on his back legs.

walk this way

Once your dog is able to balance on his back legs, you can teach him to take a few backward steps. Simply hold a treat up high and walk towards him. In order to keep the treat in sight he will have to take a step backwards. Click and reward. Practise until he learns to balance better, and work towards getting a second step before clicking and rewarding. Gradually introduce the word 'back' just before you click. Your dog will slowly become more balanced and confident at walking backwards, but keep training sessions short as it is quite hard work for him.

tall high five

Your dog can already do a high five in a sit (see pages 98–99) and now it's time to ask as he stands tall. You will need a button clicker that can be operated under your foot, as you have to open up both hands towards your dog in a high five position. Give the 'both' command so that your dog stands on his back legs. Now hold your palms out towards him in a high five command and he should reach up and try to touch them. Click as soon as he makes contact, then reward. Practise until your dog can make contact with both your hands every time.

the superdog creep

Dogs often creep or crawl instinctively when they are watching something they would like to chase, such as a bird, or if they meet another dog and are a little uncertain whether to play with him or not. Teaching your dog to creep along on his belly, either forwards or backwards, is a very effective trick and you can use your imagination to develop all kinds of variations and different scenarios.

forward creep

1 With your dog in a down position, sit on the floor next to him and raise your knees. Use the hand that is further from the dog to lure him through your legs with a treat, saying the word 'down'. Click as he moves through and treat when he gets to the other side. Alternatively, lure him underneath a chair, clicking as he moves through and treating when he emerges.

2 Stand up and, with your dog in a down, bend forward and hold a treat to his nose, keeping his head 15 cm (6 in) off the floor. Gradually move the food away from him, repeating the 'down' command. As soon as he edges forward in the down, click and reward. Introduce the command 'creep' as your dog is moving. Gradually increase the distance by clicking and treating after two or three steps rather than every one. Eventually you should be able to stand up and cue the move simply from the verbal command.

backwards creep

super tip!

Creeping can be quite demanding physically for your dog, and if he seems reluctant to stay down or keeps getting up during the move he may not be happy doing it, so watch his back legs to check for any problems such as stiffness. Your dog will always be happier creeping on a non-slip, comfortable surface such as a carpet rather than on a cold, slippery tiled floor.

1 It is easier to teach your dog to creep backwards by starting him in a bow. Kneel down and hold out a treat towards his nose. Move it steadily towards him and downwards at a 45-degree angle, as if you are putting it between his front legs. Aim to bring his nose down and back up. You don't want him to drop into a down, so as soon as he hinges back even slightly click and treat.

2 Repeat until your dog gradually lowers his elbows to the ground, then click and reward. Introduce the 'bow' or 'bend' command. Practise until you can stand and cue the move from a verbal command or hand signal.

3 Put your dog in a bow, then hold a food treat low by his nose and push it towards him, giving the 'back, creep' command. Keep your dog's nose close to the ground and as he shuffles back click and reward for a single step, then gradually build up the number of steps.

remote control

The television remote control never seems to be at hand when you want it, but that's no problem when you have a superdog! Make your life easier by training your dog to bring the remote to you on command. This is really an adaptation of the 'fetch' command (see pages 58–59), and is particularly easy to teach gundogs, such as Labradors and Golden Retrievers, who have naturally 'soft' mouths and are keen to bring you things.

fetch!

1 Get your dog used to having the remote control in his mouth by gently placing it in his jaws and clicking, rewarding and praising as soon as he holds it there. Repeat this several times so that he is confident with holding the remote.

2 Now put the remote onto a flat surface such as a table and click your dog for sniffing it. Leaving the edge of the remote hanging over the table edge will encourage him to pick it up in his mouth – then you can click, take it from him and reward. Introduce a command such as 'remote' so your dog knows what to pick up.

Confusing commands

Commands can be very confusing for your dog if they sound too similar. For example, the commands 'bed' (as in 'go to your bed') and 'beg' (sit and offer both front paws) may be difficult for him to differentiate, so it may be better to change the 'beg' command to 'please'.

Be creative with the commands you choose. With this quite complex trick, use the word 'remote' or 'telly' so that your dog knows what you want him to fetch.

If your dog has been taught to retrieve correctly (see pages 58–59) he will not crunch up the remote. The principles are the same for retrieving any article.

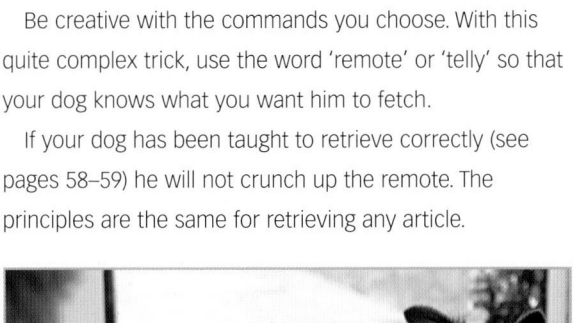

super tip!

Encourage your dog to hold the remote gently. When offering it to him, don't hold it up high so that it drops too far into his mouth, as this may encourage mouthing. The 'leave it' command (see pages 36–37) will ensure he knows to let go of the remote when asked.

3 When your dog is confidently picking up and holding the remote on command, hold out your hand to see whether he will put the remote into it. If he successfully puts the remote in your hand, click and reward. If he drops it on the floor or misses your hand wait to see if he picks it up again.

4 Gradually increase the distance between yourself and the remote control, then give the 'remote' command and click as your dog picks it up, offering him a treat when he puts it into your hand. Once your dog is confidently retrieving the remote, keep increasing the distance until he will fetch it from anywhere in the room.

canine concierge

It's a fun idea to teach your dog to open and close doors. This is quite a complex move that may take a few sessions to train successfully. Remember that you're training a superdog: he will understand that this trick can work on any door, so you need to check that he can't let himself in and out of the house when you're not around. You should make sure the handle and door mechanism moves freely enough for your dog's weight to press it down. Of course, only dogs of a certain size can do this trick.

open...

1 Refresh your dog's 'touch' (or 'tap') command (see pages 96–97) by sitting him in front of you, presenting your open hand and giving the command. As soon as his paw rests on your hand, click and give him a treat.

2 Once he's focused on this command, move to the door and place your hand beside the handle. Give the 'touch' (or 'tap') command. An average-sized dog will have to jump up on his hind legs to reach. Again, as soon as his paw touches your hand, click and reward.

3 After a number of goes, move your hand out of the way so that his paw rests on the handle. Click this immediately. At first he may not understand that the handle is the target and not your hand, but he'll soon catch on.

4 The weight of your dog's paw should push the handle down and open the door. He may be a little uncertain about this due to the unstable nature of the door handle, so reassure and praise him. Once the door is open, give him the command 'open'.

...and close

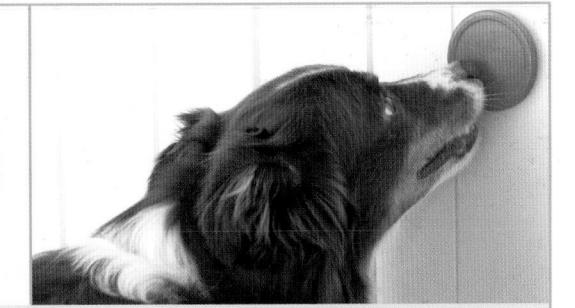

1 You can also teach your dog to close the door, using a plastic container lid as a target disc. Present this to him and as soon as his nose touches it, click and reward. After a few successful attempts attach the target to the door and give the command 'push'. Click and reward as soon as he starts to push the door.

2 Repeat this several times, each time gradually delaying the click until the door is fully shut. When he's confident in shutting the door you can introduce the command 'shut'.

winning ways

Dogs have such a highly developed sense of smell that it is relatively easy to teach them to work out which of your hands holds a tasty treat. However, if your superdog has successfully learned the retrieve (see pages 58–59) he might even manage to pick out your lucky lottery numbers for you. I would love to hear from any lucky reader whose dog is successful with this trick!

which hand?

1 Turn your back to your dog, put a treat in one hand and swap it backwards and forwards. Turn back to face your dog, then hold out both hands, saying 'get it'. As your dog already knows to give a paw by touching your hand (see pages 96–97), he will associate the words 'get it' with trying to get a treat from your hand. Allow him to sniff both your hands.

2 Keep both hands closed until your dog makes his final choice, then open your hand and give him the treat. If he chooses the wrong hand, simply keep it closed until he tries again. You can develop this trick further by using another object that can be hidden easily in your hand, such as a silk handkerchief or a small toy. Simply rub the hanky or toy with a strong-smelling treat and wrap it up tightly in your hand – just don't allow your audience to see you applying the smell!

lottery winner

1 We've all dreamed of winning the lottery and now it's time to see if your dog has a lucky streak! First make yourself a set of number cards printed with however many numbers you need. You can print these on a computer or write them with a marker pen. If you intend to use the cards several times, it may be helpful to laminate them. Folding the cards in half will make it easier for your dog to pick them up. Put your dog in a sit and wait, then lay out the number cards on the floor in a random pattern as he watches you. When you've finished, give the 'fetch' command and your dog will go and fetch one of the cards for you.

2 When your dog picks up a card, click, and when he returns it to you swap it for a tasty treat. Repeat until you have your set of lucky numbers.

neat and tidy

Dogs are intelligent animals capable of learning a large number of words. You can use this to your advantage by teaching your dog to pick up named objects and tidy them away. Give his favourite toys names – such as ball, cuddle, tuggie, teddy – and use this consistently each time he plays with the toy or brings it to you. Then you can teach him to tidy the toy away into a box or basket.

First steps

To do this trick, your dog must be able to retrieve (see pages 58–59) and also be happy to hold various objects in his mouth, so choose toys that are a good size and shape for him. You will also need a toy box with a hinged lid and a small rope or cord that you can tie to the handle.

open the box

Kneel down beside the box and encourage your dog to hold the handle in his mouth, clicking as he does so. Giving the 'walk back' command (see pages 54–55) as your dog holds the handle will pull the toy box lid open. Click as he opens the box and then reward. Repeat several times, until he makes the link that pulling the handle opens the toy box and gets him a treat. You can then introduce a verbal command such as 'open the box'.

tidy up

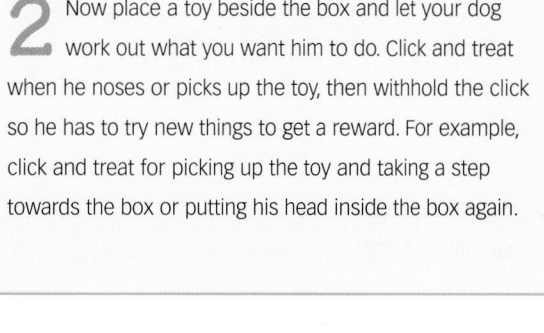

2 Now place a toy beside the box and let your dog work out what you want him to do. Click and treat when he noses or picks up the toy, then withhold the click so he has to try new things to get a reward. For example, click and treat for picking up the toy and taking a step towards the box or putting his head inside the box again.

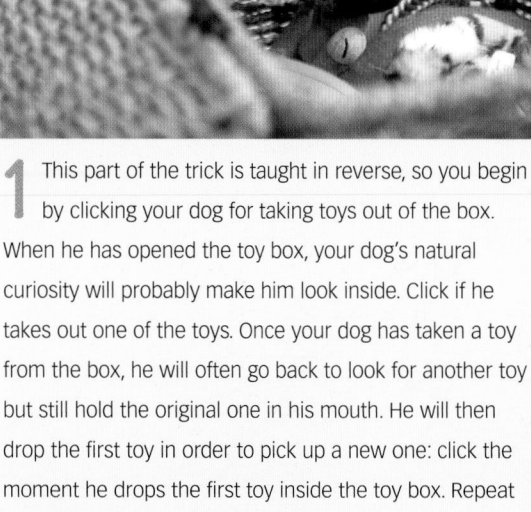

1 This part of the trick is taught in reverse, so you begin by clicking your dog for taking toys out of the box. When he has opened the toy box, your dog's natural curiosity will probably make him look inside. Click if he takes out one of the toys. Once your dog has taken a toy from the box, he will often go back to look for another toy but still hold the original one in his mouth. He will then drop the first toy in order to pick up a new one: click the moment he drops the first toy inside the toy box. Repeat several times.

3 Be patient, and gradually your dog will realize that he is being rewarded for picking up the toy and putting his head in the toy box. When he eventually drops a toy in the box, click and give a handful of treats. Continue practising and introduce the verbal command 'in the box'. If your dog recognizes some of the toys, such as a ball or teddy, you can then work on getting him to pick up specific toys and tidy them away.

quantum leap

Everyone is happy when their dog wags his tail and looks pleased to see them — so just imagine how impressive it would look if, when asked, your dog ran across the room and threw himself into your outstretched arms. Of course, this trick is not suitable for all dogs, particularly those that are older or too large and heavy for you to catch and support correctly.

teaching quantum leap

1 There are several ways to teach your dog to jump into your arms. Choose the one that suits his size and physical capabilities. The enjoyment your dog gets from doing this trick and the verbal praise he receives are usually sufficient reward and motivation for him. If you have a small dog, it's easy to put him in a sit on a chair and then encourage him to jump up at you so that you catch him. Introduce the verbal command 'up' as he jumps. If your dog is not allowed on the furniture, you could try bending down and encouraging him to jump up onto your bent knees.

Catching care

For your dog to perform this trick, he must be confident that you will always catch him and never drop him. As dogs are nearly always one-sided, you will probably find he prefers to jump into your right or left arm, so be prepared for this. When you catch your dog, take care to hold him securely and always support his back end properly.

super tip!

If your dog has always been actively trained not to jump up at you, then this is not a trick you would want to teach him as he will probably be quite reluctant to do it.

and for larger dogs...

2 Alternatively, sit in a chair and encourage your dog to jump up and sit on your lap. Gradually progress until you are standing up, but if your dog is small be sure to bend your knees to make the jump easier for him.

If you have a larger dog, you can encourage him to jump up onto something such as an armchair and try to catch him as he jumps. Make sure you are physically capable of holding and supporting your dog before you attempt to catch him. Gradually progress from him jumping up onto something until you can encourage him to jump directly into your arms, and cue the move with the verbal command 'up'. Continue practising and increase the distance between you and your dog. You can use your imagination to develop variations, and the jump can also be incorporated into a heelwork to music routine.

jumping through hoops

Hoops are available in all colours and sizes and make great props for developing superdog tricks. Use a hoop that is a suitable size for your dog and teach him to jump through it, sit in it, walk over it, and pick it up and bring it to you. Toy stores usually stock a wide range of hoops that are ideal for your dog.

hoop work

1 Hold the hoop at ground level and encourage your dog to walk through it, using a treat as a lure and clicking once his front half is through. Treat when your dog's entire body is clear. Repeat, gradually increasing the height from the ground by a small amount each time. As your dog becomes more confident, introduce the command 'hoop' or 'through' before you click.

2 Put your dog into a sit and wait. Now throw a treat or toy through the hoop, give the 'hoop' command and click as he jumps through. Eventually you will be able to dispense with the verbal command, as holding out the hoop will become a visual signal that cues your dog to jump through it. Now try adding a second hoop and holding them out in front of you a few centimetres apart, so that your dog jumps through both at the same time.

variations

1 Once your dog understands, you can develop variations, such as holding a hoop in each hand so that he jumps through each hoop and circles around you. You can also incorporate some of the other moves he has learned, such as going out on a circle (see pages 52–53).

2 Encourage your dog to hold the hoop and see what he does. My dog Tazz developed the idea of holding the hoop in his mouth and flipping it over so it landed on his back. You can also give the 'bow' (or 'bend') command (see pages 101–102) as your dog holds the hoop, or the 'both' (or 'beg') command (see pages 98–99), which looks very impressive. You can also try giving him a hoop to hold and asking for a twist, or running out on a circle.

through your arms

You can also ask your dog to jump through your arms as they form a hoop shape, but ask a friend to help you. Make your arms into a large hoop shape and bend down so they are close to the ground. Ask your helper to stand on the other side and show your dog a treat. Give the 'hoop' or 'through' command and click as your dog jumps. Your helper can then throw the treat a few paces ahead for the dog to get. Repeat several times, building up the height, clicking as the dog jumps and your helper throws a treat to keep your dog focused. Eventually you can dispense with your helper, and the visual signal of your arms forming a hoop shape will cue the move.

sweet dreams

In this cute trick your dog appears to roll over and wrap himself in a blanket, all ready for a good night's sleep. To perform it, your dog must know the retrieve command (see pages 58–59) and be happy to hold something in his mouth while he lies down and then rolls over. Teaching him to roll over holding a favourite toy first will help him understand what you want him to do.

roll over

1 To do this trick, your dog will need to understand the 'roll over' command. Begin by kneeling down in front of him and putting him in a down position. If you are rolling your dog onto his left side, hold a treat in your right hand.

2 Hold the treat close to your dog's nose and move your hand in a clockwise circle to turn his head towards his side and then up towards his shoulder. Take your time, and gradually as his head moves his hind legs will follow and he will roll over onto his side. Click when his body begins to flip to the other side and feed the treat when he has completed the roll. Practise several times in both directions, gradually building in the 'roll over' command until your dog is able to complete the move in a single, fluid movement.

good night!

super tip!

Teach this trick on a carpeted area, as most dogs will not be happy rolling over onto a cold, hard surface. If your dog only partially covers himself with the blanket as he rolls over, change where you position him on the blanket before he does the roll over to see if this produces a better effect.

1 Now you can use the 'roll over' command to develop the trick further. Spread out a lightweight blanket on the ground. Put your dog in a down position on the blanket and encourage him to hold a corner of the blanket, clicking as he does so.

2 Give the 'roll over' command as he holds the blanket in his mouth and he should take the blanket with him and cover himself as he rolls. Click as your dog rolls over and reward when he has completed the roll.

in reverse

Friends and family will be delighted with this clever trick, where your dog stands up on his back legs and does a reverse circle around them. However, your dog must first understand how to reverse on four legs around you and this is best taught using a puppy pen. Most pens are adjustable, so you can shape them easily to suit the size of your dog.

in the pen

1 Set up a pen so that your dog has only just enough room to circle around you when you are standing in the middle. Use a treat to lure him around you in a forward circle so that he becomes accustomed to the restricted space. Now put him in the left heel position and give the 'back' command, but remain stationary. If necessary, encourage him to take a step back by gently pushing a treat into his muzzle.

2 As the dog's nose emerges past your right leg, click and give him a treat on your right side. Repeat for the second half of the circle and gradually build up until your dog can complete a full circle before you click. Now withhold the click until your dog does several reverse circles. Introduce a verbal command such as 'reverse' or 'back up'. When your dog is reversing confidently, remove the pen and try without it. Practise in both directions.

Reverse on hind legs

Your dog has already learned how to stand tall (see pages 100–101), so now you can give the 'both' command, which will make him stand on his back legs. Combine this with the 'back up' command and he should reverse around you for a couple of steps. Click and reward for a couple of steps on his back legs, then gradually build up the number of steps he takes until he can can reverse around you confidently for one or more circles.

(see pages 100–101)

super tip!

If you don't have a puppy pen teach this trick using the corner of a room. Simply teach your dog to reverse half a circle each time, as he moves between you and the corner. Children love being given a chance to help with this trick and it can help to increase their confidence around dogs. Give the child some treats to hold and give to your dog after he has completed the move.

reverse around helper

1 When your dog fully understands the command, you can teach him to go to a friend and reverse around them. Tell your helper to give the 'close' command, which will put your dog into the left heel position, and then the verbal command for your dog to 'reverse' or 'back up' around them. He should do this on all fours at first.

2 Eventually, as your dog becomes more confident your helper can give the 'both' command so that your dog stands up on his back legs and reverses around them.

A superdog is ready
for anything!

FAST FORWARD

A fit, healthy dog may not retire from energetic work or competition until he is about 11 years old. However, when he gets to the age of seven or eight you should take care to do a warm-up routine before asking for anything more strenuous. This will also help to settle your nerves and get you in the right frame of mind to compete.

Warm-up routine

Start gently by walking, practising changes of direction on both sides and encouraging stretching, perhaps by asking for a bow or a stand-sit-down transition plus some twists in each direction.

Gradually increase the pace to a jog, circling your dog around you in wide circles in both directions.

Get hands on

Your older superdog will benefit enormously from regular check-ups from an animal physiotherapist or chiropractor. You may not realize he has any problems, but an experienced health professional can use massage and manipulation to make your dog's movements much freer and more comfortable.

Your dog will also appreciate you giving him a gentle massage, or you can find a health professional who specializes in canine massage.

Swimming

Gentle non-weightbearing exercise in a hydrotherapy pool is excellent for all dogs, particularly if you do not live by a safe river or pond where your dog can enjoy swimming. Five minutes of swimming can be as beneficial as 30 minutes of on-land exercise, provided the water isn't too cold and you dry him thoroughly afterwards.

Physical causes

If your dog doesn't seem to be giving his best, don't just think he's being stubborn. Seek veterinary advice to rule out a physical cause for any sudden changes in behaviour.

Safety first

An older dog can injure himself chasing after a thrown ball or toy. Modify the games you played when he was younger and consider giving him a toy and telling him to go and play instead of throwing it. You may also need to modify any tricks your dog does, such as those on his back legs, and ask him to work less overall. Finally, watch the surface you work on with your dog – if it is too slippery he may fall.

Your dog will appreciate a regular massage.

progress reports

When you are training a superdog it can be very useful to chart his progress. Knowing whether or not you are improving together can help you to maintain motivation, and will inspire you to try new disciplines and activities. If you compete with your dog and are lucky enough to win a prize this is an obvious indicator that you are doing well, but judging can be subjective and so an independent opinion is also helpful.

Video

If you have a camcorder, ask someone to video you and your dog when you are training or competing. It is not always easy to notice everything your dog is doing and

It can be helpful to watch you and your dog working on screen.

seeing you working together on screen, or from a different angle, can be a real eye-opener and will help you to identify problem areas that you can improve. This is particularly useful when you are performing a heelwork routine, as you will be focusing ahead and it is difficult to see what your dog's back end is doing.

Mirror mirror...

If you are lucky enough to be able to work in a hall with full-length mirrors, this is another great way to check how your dog is performing. Some training clubs offer this facility, so ask around to see if you can find a suitable venue.

Training clubs

One of the best ways to determine your progress is to attend a training club regularly and ask the opinion of your trainer and other dog handlers. Although I am now an experienced dog handler, I still attend a weekly class to train with other people and get my dogs accustomed to working in a room with others. Learning to concentrate when there are all the distractions of new sights, sounds and smells will benefit your dog when he begins to compete. A superdog is able to work and focus on you no matter what is going on around him.

Working around other people and dogs will also benefit you. If you become stressed or flustered when there are other people around, your dog will pick up on this and inevitably not perform as well as he would if you were calm and relaxed. Working in the informal atmosphere of a training club will help you to calm your nerves and realize that group training is a fun experience for you and your dog, which will greatly improve his performance.

Remember this

Many competitive disciplines rely on the handler's ability to remember: for example, a heelwork routine or the layout of an agility course. There are plenty of memory-enhancing computer games now available and practice makes perfect, so it may be worth investing in one or two of these and charting your own progress.

super tip!

All dogs are champions when they are working at home, but this is because they are in what they consider to be a safe, secure environment.
Learning to work well outside this comfort zone is key to becoming a superdog.

Attending a training club will help your dog become accustomed to working with distractions.

try something new!

A superdog enjoys the mental and physical challenge of trying new activities and there is no reason why you have to restrict him to one particular discipline. There are so many things you can enjoy together, and all the basic obedience work you have done with your dog in the early days can be put to good use when you try something different.

Flyball

A superdog that is brimming with energy, has a good retrieve and enjoys the company of other dogs will love flyball. This relatively new international sport is highly

Flyball dogs bounce over a series of hurdles at a high speed.

entertaining for spectators and participants alike, and competitions take place all over the world. Any breed or size of dog can do flyball, provided he is physically fit and at least one year old.

Flyball consists of a team of dogs, each of which runs over a short course of four low box hurdles. At the final hurdle, the dog's paw triggers a mechanism to release a tennis ball, which the dog catches and carries back to the starting line. The sport is fast, furious and above all lots of fun.

Check out your national canine association or the internet to find a flyball club near you, so that you can go along and watch a couple of sessions before you give it a try.

Make a splash!

A superdog that has a good recall command, is motivated by toys and loves water could excel at the new sport of Dash 'N' Splash – inspired by Dock Dogs in the USA – which in simple terms is canine long jump into water. The dog crosses a long runway above a swimming pool and a ball or toy is thrown in for him to retrieve. The aim is for the dog to jump as far into the water as possible.

Do a canine cha-cha

If your superdog has good obedience skills and you enjoy music and being creative together, you may want to try

Dash 'N' Splash is a canine long jump into water.

super tip!

Even if you don't want to compete at top level in a new discipline, your dog will benefit from trying something new. Just like people, dogs can get bored doing the same things day in day out, so explore new walks, practise new activities, go out with friends – and have fun together.

heelwork to music, either competitively or just for fun. The sport is popular all over the world and suitable for dogs of all sizes and breeds, provided you have the enthusiasm and confidence to perform.

Freestyle routines – where the dog doesn't remain in the heelwork position throughout – allow for greater creativity and you can incorporate many of the moves and tricks you will find in this book. You can wear a costume and use some props, but in my opinion dogs should not be dressed up, apart from a fancy collar or colourful neckerchief.

To find out more, contact your local dog training club or research on the internet to find a heelwork class near you. Heelwork competitions are judged in a similiar way to ice-skating competiions. The criteria are an interpretation of music, content and accuracy.

index

ackowledgements

Andrea McHugh would like to say that it was a pleasure working with Mary Ray again on her *Superdog* book, and to spend time learning some of her fantastic techniques. Behind every superdog there is a super trainer, and they don't come any more special than Mary.

The author and publisher would like to thank Bernadette Bay of the O'Bay Shetland Sheepdogs for her help and advice about early neurological stimulation. Also, thanks to all those who took part in the photoshoot:
Tippy, Zac, Saffy, Levi, Ozzy, Gypsy, Taz, Foxy and Rooney.

Executive Editor Trevor Davies
Senior Editor Charlotte Macey
Executive Art Editor Darren Southern
Designer Janis Utton
Senior Production Controller Manjit Sihra
Picture Researcher Jennifer Veall

Special photography:
© Octopus Publishing Group/Russell Sadur

Other photography:
Ardea/John Daniels 26
Octopus Publishing Group Limited/Janeanne Gilchrist 125; Russell Sadur 18, 22, 23, 25, 27, 29, 121
Steve Collins/momofoto 124 top left
The Kennel Club Picture Library 124